BROKEN DREAMS, FULFII

'Picking up this book I'm sure you'll find, as I did, that it's difficult to put down again. Carolyn and Johan's story is not only down to earth, beautifully told and hugely compelling it's also deeply humbling. There are a wealth of lessons to be learnt from their journey and the example they set by their determination to submit to, trust in, and serve the Lord. Theirs is an inspiring testimony to the fact that no matter how tough things get, those who trust in the Lord will not be put to shame!'

Mike Pilavachi, Soul Survivor

'Pain is something that we, as Christians, seldom talk about, but this amazing story of a family, walking with their friend Jesus, in the midst of great pain and difficulty, is a "must" read for us all. You will see life differently after reading this book.'

Laurence Singlehurst, YWAM/Cell UK Ministries

To Johan.
My precious, valiant husband.
Thank you for not giving up hope.

Broken Dreams, Fulfilled Promises

CAROLYN ROS

LIFE JOURNEY®

Bringing Home the Message for Life

Kingsway Communications

EASTBOURNE

ISBN 1 84291 250 X
ISBN 978 1 842912 50 8

1 2 3 4 5 6 7 8 9 Printing/Year 10 09 08 07 06

Life Journey is an imprint of
KINGSWAY COMMUNICATIONS LTD
Lottbridge Drove, Eastbourne BN23 6NT, England.
Email: books@kingsway.co.uk
Printed in the USA

Contents

Acknowledgements

To all the pilgrims who have journeyed with us along the way, for longer or shorter periods of time – our lives would not have been the same without you.

To the many friends who took the time to read the first rough draft, thank you. Your insights and comments gave me the fuel I needed to carry on.

To the two very special craftswomen who have the gift of being 'wordsmiths'. A very special thank you to Christine Terrasson and my daughter Roechama for the many hours of tinkering that they put into this manuscript to make it a book. Though their contribution is invisible to the reader, the author knows that the book is better for it. She hopes that they do, too.

It is with a sense of deep gratitude that I would like to thank my family for cheering me on in this process of writing a book, even long before there were any words on the pages. Your kindness, love and prayers have carried me. Thank you for loving me so well.

Foreword

Every person's life is a story.

The story you are about to read is unlike any story you have ever come across. It is filled with pathos and pain, grace and glory. It is so easy to say those words, but the journey that Carolyn and Johan have been on is so remarkable that words can hardly describe it.

In the middle of this story, and mixed all through it from beginning to end, you see the hand of the Creator, intervening, but not interrupting, going with them, empowering them, but not rescuing them from the mystery and discovery of His presence with them.

It won't take very many pages for you to be drawn in to this family's amazing journey. Open your heart, for you are about to see God at work in frail, faithful lives. The pain that Johan has suffered is deep, and the grace that he and Carolyn discovered together, as they opened their lives to walking by faith and not by sight, is incredible.

There are truths here, truths for every person. I plead with you not just to be drawn in to the drama of their life, but to see the truths woven through the fabric of their story.

It is my hope for you, as it happened for me, that your eyes will be opened and you will see.

Floyd McClung

Foreword

There are just a handful of families around the world whose homes I always consider it a joy and a privilege to enter. Johan and Carolyn Ros are among these. They are gentle, loving, welcoming, prayerful people, and they and their children have created, on the Romeinsarmsteeg in the very heart of Amsterdam, a place of genuine peace in a challenging city.

Broken Dreams, Fulfilled Promises will tell you at just what cost this peace has come. It is a remarkable human story of the power of faith in the face of adversity, and of the certainty of the promises of God. If you've ever wondered why God allows troubles to come into our lives, and whether anything redemptive can come from the tragedies that befall us, read this book. By the time I reached Carolyn's suggested 'pillars' for the life of faith in our world today, I was utterly gripped. Carolyn and Johan have followed the God who gives beauty for ashes and the oil of joy for mourning: and you will find him here, threading these pages with the gold of grace.

Gerard Kelly

Preface

Have you ever thought what it would be like to have the tears that you have shed wiped dry? Has it ever occurred to you what life would be like when the deep, unbearable, gaping wounds of the past are only faint scars because of the thorough healing that has taken place?

You are invited on a journey; a pilgrimage of the heart. There are many lives that share the way, some briefly, some for years, but each one has a part in shaping the path of this unfolding story.

It is not a story that runs smoothly to a climax, from low to high, and ends neatly. It is a story of brokenness; of health and youth and life shattered into fragments. It is a story of hope against hope; of tears and sadness; of doubt and fear; of discovery and new horizons.

There is nothing extraordinary about the pilgrims. They are an ordinary young couple, filled with dreams, a destiny and a calling. They wanted to make a difference in this world. The choices that they would have to make seemed exceedingly small and insignificant. However, time – yes, that precious gift called time – would show that what seemed small and insignificant had far-reaching implications.

Life is lived one breath at a time. Choices are made one decision at a time. The invitation to come and share in their pilgrimage is before you.

Carolyn Ros

Call to me and I will answer you and tell you great and unsearchable things you do not know.

(Jeremiah 33:3)

1
Faith

The family portrait in its beautiful gold frame slipped from the hospital nightstand and crashed to the floor. Pieces of glass flew in all directions. I had tried to catch it as it fell, but it slipped through my fingers. Lying mangled at my feet, the splintered glass seemed to portray all too poignantly my life at that moment.

I was sitting in Intensive Care. My husband was now beyond my reach, even though he was lying inches from me in a sterile white bed. As I gazed at the fragmented pieces of the photo frame, my mind started to wander back.

* * *

Life held so many bright promises and dreams. We had both committed our lives to serving God when we were teenagers. We had met as young adults and throughout our friendship, courtship, engagement and marriage, our one desire was to serve the Lord through training and mentoring the younger generation.

Various opportunities had opened up for us to meet that desire. We started our marriage in Japan where we taught Japanese students at a language school for two years. From there, we returned to Johan's homeland, the Netherlands, to serve in the rough-and-tumble setting of a drug rehabilitation centre. Our next challenge came after two more years, as we took on the leadership of an exploding youth work at a growing Dutch church. And here we felt that we were right where we were supposed to be. We had found our niche in life. Or so we thought.

We had known our fair share of challenges along the way. One of the earliest and most significant came after our first year of marriage while we were still in Japan, when our firstborn son Jozua was six weeks old. We suddenly noticed little bruises on his hands and feet. As new parents we were not unduly concerned; perhaps this was normal! Fortunately he was scheduled for a regular check-up at the doctor's at that time.

The check-up was scheduled early in the afternoon and as Johan was at work I went to the hospital by myself. I was not quite prepared for the Japanese doctor's response. He took one look at our son and suddenly started talking fast. He spoke in broken English, but I caught the word 'haemophilia'. Jozua was rushed off to the lab where tests showed that he had only a 12 per cent coagulating factor in his blood, and he was bleeding internally. By the time the tests were actually conducted, the doctor discovered that he was even bleeding from his palate. He was in a life-threatening situation.

My heart sank. I panicked. Johan joined me as soon as he could. How could our precious baby be dying? From his conception we had dedicated our son to God and had prayed daily for God's blessing to rest on his life. How could it end like this?

Due to the bleeding from his palate, the doctors advised us to hospitalise Jozua. An appeal was made to the international blood bank for blood for a transfusion, as he had a rare blood type that was not available in Japan. We got word that it would take days for the blood plasma to arrive. We had permission to stay at the hospital, although our son was in a separate unit with 24 small beds. All of these babies had some serious birth defect. Every three hours I went into the ward to nurse him. As I pushed my way through the heavy double doors into the ward, I could not stop weeping. I cried not only for my precious boy, but for the other little bundles of humanity who had been born into such broken bodies.

There were many nurses in the sterile ward checking up on the little ones under their care. The fluorescent light mixed with their muffled voices and the groaning of babies made this place, which was supposed to represent love and care, cold and stifling. There was a window through which I could look into another part of the ward. The infants who lay there had even more serious defects than the ones surrounding my son. The sight of all the little blinking lights from the machines that were connected to their incubators terrified me. How could God bring any redemption out of this situation? Battling to stay focused, I felt a suffocating sense of doom, like a thick cloud of poisonous gas, defiling the oxygen I tried to breathe.

At the end of this first day we were both drained and exhausted as we sat by Jozua's bed just a bit longer before having to say goodbye for the night. How could we go on? This was just one day and all our reserves already seemed to be used up. While I mused on this thought, the word 'relinquishment' reverberated in my heart. How could I relinquish my son, when I so desperately wanted to keep him, to mother him, to see him grow? There was deep agony in my heart when I looked at this seemingly hopeless situation.

How could I let him go when he was such a symbol of hope and the fulfilment of our dreams?

My husband was three when his father died. Becoming a father himself was such a powerful channel of healing for him.

How could we just let go?

We had gratefully received Jozua from God's hands, so we knew he was His, not ours. Now here he lay, in one of 24 miniature cubicles in this ward of pint-sized angels. These babies were more like celestial butterflies destined to see eternity before they'd had a chance to spread their wings. With tears streaming down our cheeks, we leaned over our son's little bed and prayed.

'Jesus, he is Yours. First and foremost, he is Yours. We so wanted him as our own. We so wanted to see him grow and find the destiny that You had for him. We wanted to see him marry and to know his children, but we relinquish our rights to him. He is Yours first and foremost. Thank You for the days that You have given him to us to enjoy. Thank You for letting us hear his first gasp of breath. Thank You for the incredible privilege of co-creating with You in a new life. Even now, his life was not lived in vain. We were able to see just a little bit more of Your sunshine and joy through his birth. Thank You for allowing us to love him. Thank You for teaching us how to dream dreams that go further than just ourselves. Thank You for the incredible miracle of seeing new life. But first and foremost, he is Yours.'

After our hearts had been poured out and it seemed that all the tears we could ever cry had been shed over our little son, we trudged back to the hospital guest-room for the night.

We slept deeply, but in the middle of the night we both sat up suddenly in bed with an incomprehensible urgency. We turned to each other and gave voice to what had awakened us: 'We must pray for our son's healing.'

Although we believed theoretically in healing and that God could do anything and everything, we were at a loss to know how to pray specifically for our son's blood to be restored to a normal coagulation level.

There is a prayer which goes deeper than speaking; a cry from the heart that needs only a few words to do the job. Our prayer could not have been longer or any more complicated than 'Lord, help!'

As we appealed to the One who alone holds eternity in His hands, hope was born. Deep down we knew that something was happening. There was a sense of jubilant expectancy that destiny had been rewritten.

I nearly ran to the ward for the next feeding. Initially, no outward sign of improvement or change was visible, but there were no new bruises. By the second and third feedings, the bruises were already a shade of yellow, a wonderful sign that they were healing normally.

Within 48 hours, all of the blood tests were repeated. This time it was the doctor, emerging from the lab, who was in a state of shock. The test readings showed 100 per cent coagulation.

With tears of joy streaming down our cheeks, we shared that we had prayed to the God of the Bible. And it was at

that moment that the significance of our son's name penetrated our hearts, for *Jozua* means 'Salvation is from the
Lord'.

* * *

Having had this experience of God intervening first hand,
the present still seemed to hold some perspective and hope.
God had healed our son. It was like a foundation stone of
faith in our lives. He had done it before. He could do it
again.

Weren't these encounters with the supernatural given as
an encouragement to believe for the impossible?

Even though I walk through the valley of the shadow
of death,
I will fear no evil, for you are with me.
(Psalm 23:4)

2

Facing Fear

Sitting at Johan's bedside, it was a hard discipline to resist fear and hold on to the promises that God had given in the past. Looking at my husband who, still not fully conscious, was just awakening after a 13-day anaesthetic-induced coma, apprehension and hope wrestled together inside me. Dare I look to the future without him? Dare I look at the present with him as he was? I relived the last two months leading up to this moment.

* * *

We were living in Soest, a small Dutch town, in a typical three-storey townhouse with a small garden at the front and another at the back. We had a very active life and three young children. Johan, my husband, was a strong and healthy person who rarely even suffered from a common cold.

Early one chilly January morning, when Johan came to the breakfast table, I noticed that his left eye was half open and he seemed to have no control over his eye muscle. Even though at that moment he was not in much pain, I knew that something was very wrong, very wrong indeed.

Panic, premonition of disaster, a gaping abyss of unbearable feelings, flooded my spirit. More questions than answers raced through my mind. What could be the cause of this paralysis in his eye?

An appointment was made with our family doctor, who wasted no time, but sent Johan to the nearby hospital for further tests. These tests showed that more specialised research was needed. Within two weeks, a slot opened up at the Academic Hospital where a CAT scan was made. The scan showed a tumour pressing on the optic nerve in the left hemisphere of the brain, right above the spinal column. The initial diagnosis was that it was inoperable and he was given two to three months to live.

Incredulous fear descended upon me. How could this be happening? Why was this happening? Had we not loved God and served Him with our lives? Had we not lived a life of purposeful investment? Had we not sought Him in the dark challenges which had come our way, and tried to honour Him in all we did?

When our visas for Japan had been up for renewal we had prayed and asked God for direction for our lives. Johan was a Dutchman with Scottish roots, I was an American with Norwegian roots and we now lived in Japan, so there were many natural options that we could pick from. We believed, though, that God wanted to tell us where He wanted to use us. While we were praying we had an impression that we were to come to the Netherlands. The Lord promised that He would pour out His Spirit on that nation and the continent of Europe. He said that He wanted to prepare us for that outpouring.

As we considered this, people started giving us Scripture verses that confirmed what we sensed in our hearts. During this time there was also a revival going on in East Timor. We had heard about this, since my parents worked with an international mission in Japan that had missionaries spread across the Pacific. We were very encouraged by the testimonies that came from that region, and by the many books we had read about great leaders of the faith and some of the revivals they had led. We believed God could do the things He had spoken to us about. When we got to the Netherlands, after having spent some months with my family in the States, we heard from others that they had also received the same impression from the Lord. This had filled us with focused zeal and clear purpose.

How could death possibly fit into this equation? We reminded the Lord of His faithfulness in the life of our son Jozua. We asked Him to heal Johan so that we could get on with life. Of course we believed in miracles. Had we not already been witness to one in the past? *'Come on, Lord; just do another miracle for us.'*

We were sure that it would be just a matter of time before all this was over and we were back to normal. But the Lord remained silent. After a period of stillness, in the agony of my soul, these were the only words of consolation that I heard: *'This is life. I want to teach you through this; stay very close to Me. Even though you walk through the valley of the shadow of death, you will fear no evil. . .'*

I did not want to hear any more. No, it could not be true that the Lord would lead us through *that* valley. I must have heard it wrong, because God is a God of love, isn't He? What could there possibly be in that valley that He could not teach us on the mountaintop? I love mountains, so that imagery spoke volumes to me. *'But not the valley, Lord.'*

His only words were, *'Stay close to Me.'*

This was the beginning of a journey to the depths of my spirit, learning what it means to stay close to the Lord in the face of fear, dread and impending evil.

During this time, something very unusual took place which would prove to be a source of great encouragement in the days that were ahead of us. One night before Johan went to the hospital, the Lord Himself gave him an experience that was going to be very crucial. He had awakened with an excruciating headache. The pain was so severe that Johan thought he could not survive it. He called out to the Lord for help. Somewhere between waking and sleeping, Johan had a vision of a storm. He was in a little boat and recognised Jesus sleeping on the rear deck. Though the hurricane-force winds were terrifying, in his vision Johan decided not to wake Jesus up, but to go back on the deck and lie down beside Him. As he did so, he felt Jesus stretch out His arm and pull him close to Himself. The storm continued to roar, but when Johan awoke there was a supernatural peace within him which could not be explained, except to say that he had been in the presence of the only One who can calm the tempest.

In this period of uncertainty over whether he could be operated on or not, Johan and I had significant heart-to-heart talks. We were told by the doctors to write out our plans for Johan's funeral, as it was very uncertain how much time he had left. No surgeon had as yet been found who would dare attempt such a risk-filled operation. As I visited each day, the gravity of his situation became clearer.

Towards the middle of February, a neurosurgeon was

located who was willing to attempt the surgery, but with no guarantee that Johan would even survive the process.

I could hardly bear the thought that my husband, so loved and cherished, might not be around to grow old with me. We still had so many unfulfilled promises for our lives. Where was the revival that we had heard was coming and of which we would be a part? What about the other promises onto which we were holding?

After the birth of Jozua, it had taken nearly five years for our next child to be born. During those years of barrenness and endless fertility tests, the Lord had given me a vision of us as a family with three sons and one daughter. At last the cause of the problem had been discovered and dealt with and our daughter Roechama was born. She was without question a daughter of destiny. Her name means 'God will show compassion'. A year and a half later we were blessed with a second son named Judah. His name means 'The Lord is to be praised'. His birth brought great joy. But where was the fourth child of promise?

The evening before Johan's operation, various spiritual leaders in the country came to his bedside to pray. There was a sense of expectancy that something significant was going to happen. I could not help imagining what miracle or wonder was going to take place to get us out of these circumstances and back to our life of action and fruitfulness.

Johan was a youth pastor of a dynamic, enthusiastic group of teenagers and young adults. He was also the dean of a Bible school and led a church home group. His training had been as a hydraulic engineer and he had gone through the Dutch Commando training (equivalent to a US Navy

Seal or British Marine) before going off to Bible school. These were very high energy, leadership positions which brought much acclaim. As his wife, it was very comfortable for me to grow in the shadow of this mighty tree. I did my part in mentoring, coaching and teaching. It just seemed that it should have gone on like that for ever.

Why did we have to look death in the face, the contours of which shook every unresolved issue that I had inside me?

On 22 February a very complicated, five-hour operation took place. Part of Johan's skull had to be removed in order to get to the deeply embedded tumour. A segment of the brain matter was cut away, but there was no malignancy. When the neurosurgeon called to give me his report, he said that he expected Johan to regain consciousness by the next day.

The next day came, and a comatose sleep enshrouded him. Breathing became more difficult and, within hours, life support was given to battle the pneumonia which was beginning to fill his lungs.

By day four, Johan's breathing had become extremely laboured. Half of his beard and curly hair had been shaven for the extra tubes and drips. It was during the visiting hour, while I was there with him in the Intensive Care Unit (ICU), that the seizures started. Violent, merciless earthquake-like shocks sent his bed and the life support equipment rolling over the ICU floor. Panic broke out among the medical staff on duty as everything in the room was moving. Though Johan was still in a coma, valium and other sedatives were given – but without results. After a short deliberation, the supervising doctor called in the anaesthetist to induce a deeper sleep, hoping in this way to prevent rupturing the incision. The brain had had a major trauma and it was assumed that this would enable the tissue to mend better.

* * *

I was jolted back to reality. Johan motioned for water. I was overjoyed to have a sign of life. Now I was sure he had come through the valley. Within weeks, he would be back to normal.

Then I looked deeply into his pale blue eyes and a sense of nausea overtook me. That glint of recognition, that spark of knowing was nowhere to be seen. One eye was still as yet half shut.

I wanted to tell him that I loved him and that I had tried to remain brave for him. I wanted him to know how we were praying for him and that we were looking forward to him coming home. I wanted to say that I planned to fix his favourite foods and how incredibly happy I was that he had made it. In my mind I was chattering away, bubbling over with all the things that I wanted to say.

But there was no recognition. Silence hung in the room like a shroud. Even a newborn baby's eyes held more recognition than I could see in Johan's eyes.

How do you call someone back to life who is living? What would the future hold for us? How do you continue to live with someone who doesn't know you any more? Would there ever be a day when I could rest in his love and acknowledgement again?

Apprehension flooded my spirit, pushing aside the faint glimmer of hope that had been there just moments before, and pressing me into despair. There was a void that had to be crossed. At that moment the promises that God had given did not seem strong enough to carry me through. The pieces of the broken picture frame still lay on the floor. Almost overwhelmed by the weight of despair, I picked up the fragments of glass and wondered if this represented what our life had become.

*The L*ORD *is close to the broken-hearted*
and saves those who are crushed in spirit.
(Psalm 34:18)

3

Eternity

As the days progressed, it became increasingly obvious that Johan seemed unable to recognise who I was and his vocabulary was fragmented and sketchy. Conversation was extremely limited. I tried to be courageous, but could not share with him the emotional rollercoaster ride on which I had been.

Our three little darlings missed their father. He had always been their big buddy and the kids were overjoyed when I could finally take them to the hospital for a visit. Expecting recognition, their young hearts could not absorb the shock of their father's mental absence. Physically, he had been reduced to a shadow of what he had been. Not only was his eye still paralysed, but also the fluid around the wound had swollen his skull, leaving a strange protrusion on the side of his head. He was able neither to comprehend what the children were saying nor to understand emotionally that they were hungering for his recognition. At that moment, he could not fathom that he was their father.

The need to be known for who we are is deeply ingrained

in our humanity. Not to have this level of knowing admin-
isters a death-blow to a relationship. How do you pick up
the fragments and make the picture whole again?

Towards the end of March, I was told that I could take
Johan home to recuperate. He was not given any form of
rehabilitation, as it was still uncertain how he would be or
if he would even survive. He had developed embolisms in
his lungs and was on thrombosis medication along with an
anti-epileptic medication, which was not doing its job.

Yet, within weeks of being released from the hospital, the
paralysis left his eye and the unseemly lump on his head
diminished. Miracles were happening!

In the early months, there was a sense of purpose: *'We will
get through this.'* However, as the months dragged into sea-
sons, the reality was that Johan had returned to us more like
an autistic child, and without any prognosis of improvement.

Table manners and basic protocol needed to be relearned.
Dinnertime conversation had become next to impossible.
His vocabulary was limited to approximately 100 words,
and what he knew was very fragmented. It was as if he had
no emotions. What I desperately tried to do was engage his
mind to capture word pictures. I did not know how to
trigger a response. I tried to coax and prod, but to no avail.

During these months, we had wonderful friends that
faithfully stood around us in prayer. One of our friends had
had a vision while she was praying for Johan. Unbeknown
to her, it was around the same time that Johan started to
have seizures in the ICU. In this vision, she saw how Johan
had passed into the presence of the Lord, but that he had
been sent back again with a commission to fulfil here on
earth. Even though we could not check with Johan to see if

this had been the case, it was a great comfort to me. It reminded me of 2 Corinthians 4, where it says we are not to lose heart even though outwardly we may be wasting away, because inwardly we are being renewed day by day.

One day one of our neighbours came by for a visit. She asked me a very pointed question: 'If Johan doesn't know your name, does he still know who Jesus is?'

This was a very scary thought. I did not know the answer. Conversation had been so difficult that we had not been able to discuss this matter before. What if he didn't know? Having him not know who I was or who the children were was devastating enough . . . dare I risk finding out that he also did not know his Saviour any more? I couldn't bear the thought.

After long, aching prayers and terrifying restlessness, I decided to ask him anyway.

From a world not of his own making, there was a sudden clarity of speech and coherency which utterly amazed me. *'Jesus is the Son of God,'* was the powerful answer. No more, no less.

My heart ached with joy. Relief penetrated my whole being with this ray of hope. At least he still knew his Creator! I marvelled at the force of that one statement. From a region deep within his spirit, almost bypassing his broken mind, came the words that have changed the course of history for the last 2,000 years. No operation, coma, epilepsy, medication, brokenness or aphasia could rob Johan of the only anchor he had that would keep him from drifting into oblivion.

Was his clear awareness of Jesus part of knowing that? Had this 'knowing' come from having been in His presence, the presence of the only One who really counts, the Creator above all else, the One who not only created but loved so deeply that He gave, gave the gift of life itself?

It helped me to realise that something was transpiring here that was of another world. The world I knew and lived in seemed so permanent, all-encompassing and definitive. How could I not plot my course by the things of the visible world? However, here was a word from a world which can only be seen or fathomed from the perspective of eternity. In that dimension, Johan's spirit was alive and well. He had returned with a mark of the Spirit upon his spirit. Would I acknowledge that this was enough, to just know Him?

There was something that began to take shape in my heart. In studying the Word, it became clear that there is an eternity and what happens during our lifetime will have bearing on what will come. I began to contemplate what was taking place within Johan's spirit and what that had to do with life as I knew it now. Again 2 Corinthians spoke to me.

Therefore we do not lose heart. Though outwardly we are wasting away, yet inwardly we are being renewed day by day. For our light and momentary troubles are achieving for us an eternal glory that far outweighs them all. So we fix our eyes not on what is seen, but on what is unseen. For what is seen is temporary, but what is unseen is eternal.

Now we know that if the earthly tent we live in is destroyed, we have a building from God, an eternal house in heaven, not built by human hands. Meanwhile we groan, longing to be clothed with our heavenly dwelling, because when we are clothed, we will not be found naked. For while we are in this tent, we groan and are burdened, because we do not wish to be unclothed but to be clothed with our heavenly dwelling, so that what is mortal may be swallowed up by life. Now it is God who has made us for this very purpose and has given us the Spirit as a deposit, guaranteeing what is to come.

(4:16–5:5)

In this portion of Scripture, we are told not to lose heart. Even though this fleshly body is wasting away, a renewal in the inner man is taking place. There is a shift of focus from what is seen to the invisible world, which is the true reality. The ensuing verses tell of the longing to be with the Lord, but while still on earth to be faithful to Him.

There it was in black-and-white print for me to read: the Holy Spirit has been given to us as a pledge, a down payment of what is to come. Even though Johan's mind could not comprehend what he had said, his spirit had spoken out of the reality of what it is to be known by the Father. The operation had not touched his spirit.

I wanted to grasp this truth with my heart. More was transpiring before my eyes than I could immediately fathom.

The Lord *was* in our midst. I still could not comprehend why we were on this journey, but He was with us. Through Johan's short response, the Lord spoke to me from eternity, reminding me that reality looks different from His perspective. The grave is not the last answer; there is more, even though a grave brings acknowledgement that a life is over from our point of view. There is life that knows no end; there is life that goes further than the grave.

I contemplated Job and his challenges, but because I was not the one who was sick, many of his struggles were hypothetical to me. What I did realise, though, was my affinity with Job's wife. Dear sweet lady, how I could empathise with her plea of despair. Losing all her children, her wealth, and her husband's position, power and health was just too much. Her charge to 'curse God and die' really isn't that absurd.

Except that I did not want to end up in that place. I realised that I had the capacity to be just like her. The frustration level within me was building with each day, each long day. The future did not exist as I would recognise it and the past was only my faint memory. How do you go on like this?

An inaudible prayer began to grow in my heart: 'Jesus, I acknowledge that I could throw in the towel and give up. My husband does not resemble the person I married. I do not know if he will ever be restored. I do not know if he will ever be able to do anything more than stare out of the window. I do not know how to give a sense of family to three young, traumatised children. To have a grave where we could take flowers would be painful, but so much easier than living with the living dead. I do not have the strength, as a foreigner, to know how to function well in this foreign country. I am lost without Johan as my guide, the one I can consult.

'Jesus, I acknowledge that I am at my end. However, please Lord, help me not to get to the point of cursing You. I embrace Your Word that says that You will not put to shame those who put their trust in Your name. I do not have a plan B. Either You help our family to get through this, or we will not make it. Give me a steadfast spirit not to give in to anxiety, fear, doubt, despair, hopelessness and depression. Open my eyes to be able to see that the visible things are only temporal but that the unseen things are eternal.'

I had to make a choice. For today, I would choose not to give up. What tomorrow would look like, I did not know. There was a promise, however: *'As my day is, so shall my strength be.'*

For our light and momentary troubles
are achieving for us an eternal
glory that far outweighs them all.
So we fix our eyes not on what is seen,
but on what is unseen.
For what is seen is temporary,
but what is unseen is eternal.
                    (2 Corinthians 4:17–18)

4

Faithfulness

About a week after Johan was discharged from the hospital, the epileptic seizures started up again. They would strike at unexpected moments, generally without warning. One day while we were shopping for groceries, I heard a thud behind me and turned around to see Johan collapsed on the floor, twitching violently. Once he lost consciousness and the spasms began, there was nothing to be done but make sure that he did not bite his cheek or tongue and wait out the storm.

The unpredictability of these grand mal attacks made life challenging. The question was, what had triggered such a drastic response in his brain? If I knew the cause, I thought it would somehow be possible to prevent the seizures. When Johan regained consciousness, his orientation and memory would be severely affected, sometimes for hours.

Several times, over the years, I have received calls from the hospital saying that a pedestrian had found him collapsed on the ground, in the middle of a seizure. An ambulance had been summoned, he had been taken to the hospital for observation, and would I come, pick him up, and take him home.

After the initial shock of having to find him in the hospital again, I was amazed to realise that something supernatural had been taking place. In the whole process of allowing Johan to go out on walks without me as his constant companion, I had had to learn to let go and relinquish my worries to the Lord. I could not protect Johan, but the Lord was showing me that He could. I have often wondered if He quickened the heart of some passer-by to give Johan first aid, or if angels had been sent to mediate and help. In either case, ultimately nothing life-threatening ever took place.

Relinquishing my concern, anxiety and worry was maybe the hardest challenge in this area of letting go. Johan could not tell me what his own limits were and I had to guess at what he was capable of handling. It felt as if I was letting him flounder and yet the only way not to give in to despair was to let go.

The battle for sanity forced me onto my knees in prayer. I was desperate in many areas, and the cry of desperation is a cry that God always hears. How was I to help Johan regain his ability in the Dutch language? As a native English speaker, I did not know how to stimulate and train his brain to rediscover the linguistic pathways in his native language. He only had basic syntax in his sentence patterns and his world revolved around the simple present tense.

I asked the Lord for a strategy, and what He gave me was remarkably uncomplicated. I was to read aloud, which I did for hours on end. I read story books, the Bible and children's stories. I went through family photo albums and retold him his own history. He had a cassette player and someone read the whole book of Romans onto a tape to which he could listen. Even though it felt awkward at first, at the dinner table I began to discuss things with the kids. They were still in elementary school, but I would ask them their opinion on different issues. I was not only interested in the 'playground' news, but I also talked with them about current events.

The silence had to be broken through, not only with empty chatter, but with meaningful words.

Over the years, one of the blessings that has emerged as a side-effect of this approach is the fine vocabulary of the children. They learned to communicate easily with each other and with adults. They were not inhibited about carrying on a conversation, as they knew that they had something worthwhile to say.

It took Johan seven months to relearn how to read. Repetition and prayer were the keys to help unlock his mind. Writing remained a challenge, so I did not attempt to conquer this at the time.

After about a year, he had regained more of a sense of family identity. Even though he continually mixed up our names, I was at least an 'aunt' or 'mother' and every so often I would regain my identity as 'Carolyn', although the concept of 'wife' was still quite abstract for him.

I had to look again at the marriage vows that we had made. We had very purposefully made a covenant before the Lord when we got married. By doing this, we were acknowledging that we needed God as part of the equation of our marriage. Our human resources seemed endless on such a day as our wedding day, but we knew enough about who we were and human nature in general to realise that we would need God's help and grace when the going got rough. We needed a Source to draw from which was bigger than ourselves. We needed God to help us remember what we vowed to each other.

Because we were married in Japan, we had had four ceremonies (the Dutch consulate, the American consulate, the Japanese city hall and a church wedding conducted by my dad), which gave us ample time to really know what we were doing!

It is easy on a wedding day to promise 'for better or for worse', but I surely did not expect actually to have to hold on to my part of the bargain 'for worse'. Yet this covenant that we had made did not allow me to 'abandon ship' just because it looked hopeless.

I remember that I asked the Lord to help me stay faithful, really faithful, walking in holiness even in the secret part of my heart. It was so hard to have memories and everyday life experiences but no one with whom I could share them. I knew enough about counselling to know that I could not make my children into my pastoral helpers.

My words would be very important and would help determine how I viewed our relationship. I knew that 'life and death are in the power of the tongue'. It was not easy to know how to speak out life and truth and not just wishful thinking over our situation. Faithfulness meant that as long as each of us had breath in us, I had to work on seeing and referring to us as a 'we'. I needed to continue to discuss my thoughts, ideas and plans with Johan while keeping a watch over my heart so as not to develop an independence from him. This was extremely difficult to do, as he had no idea that what I was doing was attempting to save our marriage.

I had wonderful friends, but there are processes in life that cannot always be shared. I could not continually call up friends to talk and try to work out everything that I was going through. I was hesitant to share Johan's inadequacies with others, as I did not want to jeopardise his being able to re-emerge, even though he was a person without a past.

In the loneliness of this period, I asked the Lord for protection over my heart. I had asked Him to help me stay faithful, emotionally and physically, but I also asked Him to teach me how to love a person who was unknown to me. Johan did not resemble the one whom I had married, and he did not understand that I wanted to be known and loved by him as well.

As time went on, this prayer began to be answered. To know someone intimately has varying depths. A slow awakening was taking place which allowed the initial steps towards intimacy to take place. It is so true that we are fearfully and wonderfully made. Even though Johan's verbal communication on a deeper level was not fully revived, there were rays of hope that encouraged me that we were still 'one' together.

But we have this treasure in jars of clay
to show that this all-surpassing
power is from God and not from us.
                            (2 Corinthians 4:7)

5

Facing Grief

S orrow knows many faces: the sorrow of broken dreams, of unfulfilled promises, of death itself. I had not realised that this could also apply to life.

A life that goes on devoid of the landmarks that had characterised it as unique and special is heartbreaking. Devoid of the little whispers of sweet nothings in each other's ears; knowing, yes, knowing those little quirks that make the other burst out laughing or drive him or her up the wall. The chatter and banter that is part of the tapestry of life.

Not only do words define the silence, but they are also a medium to communicate what the speaker wants to share. The hearer chooses a response based on the boundary given by the spoken word and the knowledge of who the speaker is. Rarely, if ever, do we consider these reference points as we talk, but when they are gone, communication becomes like paddling in a rubber ring on the ocean. Direction is lost and progress is negligible.

I had to explain repeatedly the most simple words or concepts that I used. Repetition was the key, although I often gave up after several attempts, usually in a puddle of tears.

I felt guilty at not appreciating the simple accomplishments of every day. But I wanted more than just the basic words, 'I want a cup of coffee.' I did not know how to penetrate the darkness of Johan's mind to cause him to 'awaken'.

Memories do not surface in logical or sequential ways and can be a persecutor and tormentor.

I still remember well the first time that I saw Johan. It was at the Bible college in northern England where we were both students. I was waiting on the stairs in the foyer for the lecture room door to open. A tall, strikingly handsome young man entered the hall and sat down. His chestnut-coloured hair and beard and sparkling blue eyes made him quite a sight to behold. I had to stay rather focused so as not to allow my emotions to run away with me. I guess it's rather a girlish thing to say, but my heart skipped a beat! He had such a stately composure and presence.

It transpired that during our weekend breaks from school, he would take groups of us students on hikes through the hilly countryside of the Lake District. One of the characteristics that struck me on these hikes was that he was able to give the whole group the confidence that we needed. He convinced us that we had what it took to survive this trek! As he led us through fields, over stone walls and to a little waterfall or other scenic spot, I felt comfortable and at home with this very cheerful guide.

After finishing at the Bible college, I continued my studies at the Summer Institute of Linguistics, which was the training programme for the Wycliffe Bible Translators. Much to my delight and surprise, Johan and I found that our paths crossed again. Upon completion of the training, I was to go to Germany to work on helping with the layout for the Romanian Bible concordance. As we said our good-byes the night before my departure, Johan and I suddenly realised that our enjoyment of each other was more than a good friendship. I am not sure if it came as a bolt of lightning or fireworks or both, but I knew that this man was going to be my husband.

In the midst of the hard reality of the present, I was drawn back again and again to the memories of this dynamic, energetic man in whose giant shadow I had found such love and rest.

* * *

In any personality test that Johan had taken, he had scored highly as a strong visionary leader. He could inspire and lead and yet knew that he needed a team around himself. He understood what his weaker spots were, though it was hard for him to empathise with real weakness, as he had never had to deal with this first hand. He had the gift of making you believe that the impossible and uncharted were achievable.

He loved to do things in new ways and was very innovative. He thrived on adventure and believed that he could help train a generation of young people to break out of the mould of complacency and be radical in their commitment to God and each other.

During our time in Japan, he both taught English and helped build several churches. He loved to take Japanese Christians on outreaches to Siberia to be an encouragement to the underground church there at that time.

While working as a counsellor in the rehabilitation centre, Johan helped to instigate some programmes which, coupled with the counselling, gave the clients some hard physical labour. Cutting down damaged trees after a storm or marching 50 kilometres to train for a national walking marathon was all part of Johan's no-nonsense approach to life, and he felt that such activities would help to get these recovering addicts back on track. It was in this period of our lives that Johan was invited to join the staff of a large church and work at the Bible school connected to the church.

As a youth pastor he believed that everybody had a part to play. He definitely did not believe in spectator Christianity. Belonging meant taking responsibility for some part of the whole. A new believer was plugged in immediately, both to a Bible study group and by receiving some task. The young people thrived on this approach. Powerful memories were also made on the outreaches to countries in the former Eastern Bloc that the young people took under Johan's leadership.

The main ingredient in this exuberant youth work was prayer. For years, there was a house full of young people who would come together for prayer. This was the backbone of whatever was done during the rest of the week. Johan was known for his poignant one-liners. One of these was, 'A believer who doesn't pray is like a soldier who has a rifle without bullets.'

As dean of the Bible school, he would sometimes take the students to Amsterdam to join evangelistic outreaches on the city streets with the staff of Youth With A Mission, an international, interdenominational missions organisation. In this way, we got to know various YWAM staff members working there.

Johan had a passion to facilitate the training of his students, future pastors and missionaries, not to give up under difficulties or adverse circumstances. Little did he know that the training he gave to others was just as much for himself.

As an engineer, he loved to tinker. He could literally take a pile of scrap metal and make something useful out of it. He was an artist at heart with a flair for the flamboyant.

As a dad, he had the hearts of the children in his hands. They absolutely adored their strong oak tree of a father. He excelled in taking them on adventures into the forest to teach them survival secrets that he had learned as a Dutch Commando. The children's friends loved to tag along on these unique exploration jaunts.

* * *

I did not know how to force my thoughts to stay focused on accepting the fragmentation of now. The 'now' we lived in seemed so permanent. We had had crowds of well-wishers, but they naturally dwindled as time went on. At one point I had counted 70 plants and flower arrangements scattered throughout the house. Even the bathroom was supplied with flowering beauty! I had been able to buy a second-hand piano from the money often found enclosed in the scores of cards and letters we had received. But time moved on and I still had to face the present.

I caught myself wrestling with hope and doubt and the impossible question of why we could not simply wake up one morning and find our present life as normal as our past.

Such a fantasy was dashed to pieces as I was regularly jolted awake at night with the suffocating sounds of an epileptic attack starting. I would plead with the Lord to stop the violent shaking, the gagging, choking, gasping breath. But once Johan slipped into unconsciousness, the earthquake would take over and I had to ride it out with him. Each violent shake seemed like the last quiver of a leaf in a storm. How could his body and mind survive such jostling? My first aid always included prayer, a plea, and a request to the Creator to spare this valiant warrior, for that he was.

The next morning, Johan would generally have no recollection of what the night or the preceding hours had brought. He often had sore muscles to nurse as proof of the intruder, but it seemed as if his memory had been washed clean again, and I had to start from square one to teach him what had happened that day.

How do you really describe grief?

I would cry out to the Lord that this was too much. I could not stand to see my husband reduced to such insignificance. How could I stop these lurking, unpredictable, life-threatening intruders from returning? Not only that, how could I fall asleep again with the uncertainty that the predator might return?

In my utter desperation, I would pick up the only Word that could steady my shaken spirit. I asked the Lord for consolation. I needed comfort. There was no one to hold me and rock me to sleep with a silent song.

As tears streamed down my face, I would open the Bible at random to the Psalms. The Holy Spirit ministered life through words that jumped out of the pages at me. Over the years, these words became the confession of my heart, the proclamation of hope for just one more day, the declaration of faithfulness that my Father did see my sorrow and grief.

He cared. He was intimately concerned for my welfare and my sanity. I was known to Him.

I finally got to the place where I realised that I needed to have a burial service for the Johan I had known. It was unfair to him for me to compare him as he was now to the person he had been. I had the memories he did not. I only tormented myself by making the comparisons. It always left me with a sense of despair, as the new Johan could not compare with the one I had known.

It is rather awkward to bury someone who is still walking around, but the process took place in my heart. I needed a monument, a point of recognition that there was a past that was very different from the present. Who knew what the future would look like? As for now, I acknowledged that, essentially, the husband I had known had died. Should anything come back, it would have to be because of the resurrection power of Jesus. That possibility had to stay open.

In the living grief, there were the children to be considered. Often the focus is on the patient, maybe the spouse, but rarely do the little ones get the space to speak out their hurt and pain. It was so complicated. The shell of their father had returned, but the connection and content were missing. How do you explain this to a child who is not at the stage of objectivity and rationalisation? How could I explain that their father had not abandoned them and really did care even if he could not express it?

Each child had a different response. Jozua bottled up his grief inside himself. He had lost his buddy and, as his Mom, I just could not fill the void.

Roechama was like a little tropical shower. She would cry

until there were no more tears and then go out and play with her girlfriends.

Judah, precious tree-climbing boy, was going to conquer the world on his own without any of us helping.

My prayer, my agonising prayer, became, *'Lord, turn this into gold in their lives. My heart is crushed in grief for them but keep them from the prison of self-pity or uncontrollable anger towards You, Jesus. Hold on to them and give them hope. Hope that there is a destiny for them. Hope that life holds a promise and not just tears.'*

Do not be anxious about anything, but in everything,
by prayer and petition, with thanksgiving,
present your requests to God.
And the peace of God, which transcends all
  understanding,
will guard your hearts and your minds in Christ
  Jesus.

(Philippians 4:6–7)

6

Sustaining Prayer

Two fellow travellers supporting us on our journey were my parents. My mum had come over from the States to surround us with prayer and to help with the children during Johan's hospitalisation. She was able to be with us for a month.

This had presented challenges in communication, as we had had to switch to Dutch as our primary language when our oldest son was two years old. It was difficult for him to have English and Dutch spoken at the same time. In order to simplify the challenge and enable him to learn one language well before learning another, I had to relinquish my English for a season. The implications of this were that the children were more comfortable speaking Dutch to their American grandmother. This would have been quite complicated, had it not been for the fact that Mum had an enormous heart of love. Her Norwegian roots gave her the creativity to understand the children and enabled her to use her Norwegian to communicate with them, as both languages have a Germanic origin. The amazing thing was that they could understand her and got along fine.

(On a side note, I believe we can understand many more languages than those we have learned if there is a desire to communicate. Wanting to communicate opens up deaf ears and gives the ability to hear the heart. This is the seat of true communication, and it worked for us.)

Mum's primary contribution at this time was not her babysitting, meal preparation or fellowship, but her prayers. She was a prayer warrior. She knew how to go to battle and reach out in faith for the impossible.

She had had years of training. As a 19-year-old, she had been miraculously healed of tuberculosis of the anklebone. Together with my dad, she went to Japan, where they stayed for 30 years as missionaries, having responded to the call for missionaries to that country after World War II. As a baby I was taken to this unknown land, which I grew up knowing only as a country that I loved.

My parents pioneered and ploughed with their prayers. Their zeal was to tell the Japanese people about the unconditional love, forgiveness, redemption, reconciliation and compassion of Jesus. Prayer. Midnight prayers. Beseeching, petitioning prayers. Joyous, jubilant prayers. Yes, my mum knew whom she served and was not timid to approach the only One who could turn water into wine; mourning into dancing; make the crippled to walk again; or bring back life where death was threatening.

I learned courage from this mighty warrior. Courage is not proceeding without fear, but proceeding in spite of it. Until Mum went home to be with Jesus many years later, she remained a prayer warrior.

An early morning phone call from my dad in 2003 urgently asked me to get on the next plane to Seattle. A series of strokes had brought Mum to the edge of eternity. Although I never could talk with her again, being with her while she was in a coma before her death was a profound experience. Despite the tears, the presence of the Lord was so heavy in the room that I dared not hold on to my precious Mum when I knew the Lord was calling her home.

Back in the Netherlands after the funeral, a letter was waiting for me. Mum had written it several days before her stroke. With the time difference and the postal system being as it is, I got the letter upon my return. Her last words, speaking to me from beyond the grave, encouraged me to continue to put my trust in the Lord.

The prayers of this soldier of the faith paved a road of hope in my heart. In Japan my parents had persevered in prayer, and they had seen results. For a time it seemed that we, too, would soon see wonderful restoration and get back to the rhythm of life we had lost so suddenly. I just wanted to pick up the thread of our lives again. Why was it taking so long?

The prayer of a righteous man is powerful and effective.

(James 5:16)

7

Strategic Prayer

This journey we were on was not undertaken alone. Besides my parents, we were blessed by an army of dedicated friends who prayed. Their prayers were like gusts of fresh air, fanning that little flame of hope – hope that this was not a dead-end street but a passageway into a bigger arena. These mighty men and women poured their hearts out in prayer, asking the Lord for the impossible: healing, restoration and a future. May they always be remembered for their sacrifices to believe God can recreate and make something out of nothing. They exercised their faith and in doing so gave me courage to believe.

Even to this day, various people meet several times a year in a group that we have named 'Chavarot', a Hebrew word meaning friendship. Prayer unites hearts more than anything else can do. God would give us a strategy as to how to pray. Part of the strategy was based on the first chapter of Genesis. In this portion of the Word, we read how the Spirit of God hovered over the formless chaos at the beginning of creation. When God spoke, that which had not existed came into existence. This became the pattern of our prayers.

We would pray for Johan: for the retention of concepts, names, people, history and associations; to know his extended family; for humour; to be able to be flexible in his thoughts; to be able to see the bigger picture; for the ability to have abstract thoughts; to know his children and their particular histories; to know our neighbours; to be able to remember where he lived; to remember vacations on which we had been; to learn how to laugh again; to learn how to feel again; to learn how to cry again; to learn how to say that he needed something; to learn how to say, 'I'm sorry'; to learn how to ask, 'How are you doing?'; to learn to know me again.

Which part of the brain is coded for all these things? Only the Creator knows. Only He knew which areas needed His resurrection power.

Glimmers of hope came, and small victories. Slowly coherency began to resurface. The improvement was not always perceptible. At times, it was as if three steps forward were accomplished only to slip back two steps. Specific prayers were being answered, however, for restoration, to be able to process all the differing impulses requiring a variety of sensory responses.

It was a challenge to teach him that it was okay to say that something hurt. In this sense, pain is an ally to help prevent something worse happening.

Most people who visited us were confronted with the need to reintroduce themselves to Johan and explain how he had known them in the past. Some did not mind doing this, but others found it to be too challenging.

The children and I were in this together with Johan. It affected all of us. I had to protect my heart when letters began to arrive telling us how, if we did this or that, everything would be restored to normal. The fact that life was not back to normal was seen as a sign that something was fundamentally wrong with us. It is hard not to start to doubt your own life. Maybe there was a simple formula that we could recite to get us out of this immense valley?

At times like this, the Lord would speak His words of comfort: *'Stay very close to Me, My child.'*

Could it be that the Vine-dresser was allowing this pruning? Was He actually targeting the fruit-bearing branches? Was this why so many prayers seemed to remain unanswered? Could it possibly be that a time would come when more fruit would be produced because of the pruning?

The cry of my heart became: 'I would have despaired unless I had believed that I would see the goodness of the LORD in the land of the living' (Psalm 27:13 NASV).

You are my hiding place;
you will protect me from trouble
and surround me with songs of deliverance.
                                    (Psalm 32:7)

8

Singing Truth

There were times when my soul was so depleted that music was the only solace. The songs by Michael Card brought comfort and encouragement to my heart. I would also sing Keith Green's songs at the top of my voice while I was cleaning. All the while, tears would be streaming down my face. I felt like a mountain climber on the face of a sheer rock looking for a crack where I could pound in my peg. Each song gave hope, life-changing hope. Michael Card's 'Joy in the Journey' was one of the most significant songs during that time.

> There is a joy in the journey
> There's a light we can love on the way
> There is a wonder and wildness to life
> And freedom for those who obey
>
> And all those who seek it
> Shall find it
> A pardon for all who believe
> A hope for the hopeless
> And sight for the blind

To all who've been born of the Spirit
And who share incarnation with Him
Who belong to eternity
Stranded in time
And weary of struggling with sin

Forget not the hope
That's before you
And never stop counting the cost
Remember the hopelessness
When you were lost?

There is a joy in the journey.

(Copyright © 1986 Birdwing
Music/Mole End Music/EMI Christian
Music Publishing)

As I began to ponder what the Word had to say about 'songs of deliverance', I realised that I could partner with the Lord by engaging my spirit in music, liberating and life-giving music.

If I were a musician, it could rightfully be said that it would be easy for me to say these things, but I have the singing-in-the-shower type of talent. However, now I began to realise that this was not enough and that I needed to be bolder in how I sang. 'I will sing a new song to you, O God' (Psalm 144:9a).

Learning how to break the silence with my own song brought a release. Not because of the melodious quality of my voice, but by the power of the proclamation of truth. I did not fully understand what was transpiring, but I later learned that the speaking of truth changes your mindset, which in turn influences your actions and ultimately affects the circumstances.

One of the ways of practising this exercise of singing out songs of deliverance was by using the Psalms as my textbook. Sometimes I made up my own melodies, at other times I sang tunes composed by inspired songwriters. If my spirits were too low to strike a chord, I would put on worship music. I would allow the jubilation of others to carry me to the throne room of the Most High. Listening was not a passive experience, but an active exercise, coupled with faith in my heart.

Years ago, I read a book about a prisoner during the Vietnam War who survived his captivity, under the most horrendous circumstances, by reciting the songs that he had learned as a child in Sunday school. This not only lifted his spirit, but the truth he was repeating resulted in setting his heart free as well.

Long before Johan's operation and when the children were still very young, we had incorporated this idea into our daily family routine by singing a song of thanksgiving to the Lord after our meals. It became a tradition that we have continued with the kids ever since. In this way, music naturally grew to be part of our everyday life. But something more significant was going on. Our simple singing brought a daily proclamation of truth over our situation and ourselves, influencing the very atmosphere around us, like light, which by its very nature diminishes darkness.

Write in a book what you see.
(Revelation 1:11a nasv)

9

Feeding on Truth

S till, I was in need of a place where I could talk with total freedom and pour out all that was in my heart. I had wonderful, supportive family and friends, but in the nights when Johan had a seizure I was essentially alone. I could not wake up the children to talk to them, knowing such a burden was not appropriate for young hearts.

I asked the Lord for a solution. The thought came to mind to write down my prayers in a journal, and so I began what has become a priceless record of God's dealings with me. The verses that came to me at night were a lifesaver. Through His Word, God intervened in the dark hours to give light, hope, courage and life. Over the years, I have accumulated more than 30 of these journals. For me they represent the true pilgrimage of my soul. God could handle my doubts and fears. By recording this journey, I had a powerful testimony of the answers to prayer that inevitably came.

I would like to share some of the key verses that the Lord gave me after Johan's seizures and the meditations that grew from them.

===========================

The LORD has heard the voice of my weeping.
(Psalm 6:8b NASV)

There is a groaning of the spirit that has no words, but it speaks volumes. He hears.

===========================

The LORD also will be a stronghold for the oppressed,
A stronghold in times of trouble,
And those who know Your name will put their trust in You;
For You, O LORD, have not forsaken those who seek You.
(Psalm 9:9–10 NASV)

After each seizure, it feels as if the dykes have broken. Johan's words, concepts and memories seem to be washed away by the violent rush of water that does not leave much standing. Oh, how I need a stronghold. What is in a name? Everything! I know how my heart aches to hear Johan call me by my name. Here the Lord is inviting me to call Him by His name. This will invoke trust, as He is as good as His name. He has promised never to forsake me. Declaring this is like damming up the broken-down dykes again.

=======================

I will bless the LORD who has counselled me;
Indeed, my mind instructs me in the night.
I have set the LORD continually before me;
Because He is at my right hand, I will not be shaken.
(Psalm 16:7–8 NASV)

Oh boy, do I ever need strategy. I need help big time. How do I give identity to the family by myself? How can I impart the sense of being Dutch to Johan and the kids while being an American myself? I appeal to You, Lord, for Your counsel and instruction. Surely, You can give me the keys that I need to make this happen. I ask You for the safety and security which my heart longs for.

========================

Some boast in chariots, and some in horses;
But we will boast in the name of the Lord, our God.
(Psalm 20:7 NASV)

There are no human resources left on which to call. The only thing remaining is God's recreating power. Here is an invitation to proclaim who He is. Even though I cannot see the outcome right now, I can activate my spirit to make my boast in Him. His Word promises that He will come through with His power and His strength.

========================

For He has not despised nor abhorred the affliction of the
afflicted,
nor has He hidden His face from him;
But when he cried to Him for help, He heard.
(Psalm 22:24 NASV)

The Lord is not shocked by the extreme brokenness of our lives. He is here and He promises that we will find Him in the midst of what we are going through. Our prayers are getting through to Him. This brings profound comfort.

========================

The Lord is my shepherd, I shall not want.
(Psalm 23:1 NASV)

I feel only lack and want. It does not seem that this is applicable to me. As I make it a declaration of truth, however, my Shepherd shows me how He is caring for my every need. In fact, there are times when He provides even before I ask.

==========================

The secret of the LORD is for those who fear Him,
And He will make them know His covenant.
My eyes are continually toward the LORD,
For He will pluck my feet out of the net.

(Psalm 25:14–15 NASV)

I want to know Your secrets, Lord. How did You survive in Gethsemane? The snare of entanglement and the threat of being sidetracked was an ever-present reality for You, as it is for me. The entanglements that I face are these: the threat of giving up hope; the temptation to decide to seek my own fulfilment at the cost of others; not wanting to have to make any more sacrifices; the emotional and mental exhaustion of trying to be two parents while encouraging Johan that he is loved and valuable even when we can't get any counsel from him. Lord, You are giving me a key. You are telling me to revere You and to keep my eyes focused on You. This will enable me not to be caught in the snare of the enemy, which I so easily can see before me.

==========================

I would have despaired unless I had believed that I would
see the goodness of the LORD in the land of the living.
Wait for the LORD; be strong and let your heart take courage;
Yes, wait for the LORD.

(Psalm 27:13–14 NASV)

This has become my shout, my song, my war cry. I know what the suffocating presence of despair breathing down my neck feels like. I take this as my Magna Carta, a proclamation for tomorrow what I hope for today.

=========================

> Be strong, and let your heart take courage,
> All you who hope in the LORD.
>> (Psalm 31:24 NASV)

How can I be strong when I just want to crawl under the blanket and hide? But in the midnight hours, You speak courage and strength into my heart.

=========================

> The righteous cry and the LORD hears, and delivers them out of
>   all their troubles.
> The LORD is near to the broken-hearted, and saves those who
>   are crushed in spirit.
>> (Psalm 34:17–18 NASV)

A loved baby who whimpers at night will not be left alone. In the same way, You have heard my cry. You have heard my pitiful groaning of powerlessness. You have come near and Your comfort is like a warm blanket surrounding me.

=========================

> How precious is Your loving-kindness, O God!
> The children of men take refuge in the shadow of Your wings.
> They drink their fill of the abundance of Your house;
> You give them to drink of the river of Your delight.
> For with You is the fountain of life; in Your light we see light.
>> (Psalm 36:7–9 NASV)

My soul longs for the light. When a match is lit in a dark room, involuntarily one is drawn to the light. In the same way, Lord, Your light is illuminating my darkness. These are words of solace and refuge.

==============================

Lord, all my desire is before You;
And my sighing is not hidden from You.

(Psalm 38:9 NASV)

The Lord knows me. I do not have to try to impress Him that I have it all together. What a freedom to be able to come to Him as I am!

==============================

The LORD will command His loving-kindness in the daytime;
And His song will be with me in the night,
A prayer to the God of my life.

(Psalm 42:8 NASV)

Each day and each breath are proof of His love. His angels are singing over me in the night-time hours.

==============================

Why are you in despair, O my soul?
And why have you become disturbed within me?
Hope in God, for I shall yet praise Him,
The help of my countenance, and my God.

(Psalm 42:11 NASV)

I have to train my soul not to give in to despair. That path is well worn and needs to be neglected. A new path needs to be created, turning my focus to hope in the Lord.

========================

When I am afraid, I will put my trust in You.
In God, whose word I praise,
In God I have put my trust;
I shall not be afraid.

(Psalm 56:3–4 NASV)

I have a choice, either to give in to fear, or to acknowledge it but choose to put my trust in the Lord.

========================

You have taken account of my wanderings;
Put my tears in Your bottle.
Are they not in Your book?

(Psalm 56:8 NASV)

My tears and sadness are not unseen. An account is being kept of the journey of my soul. This brings an enormous comfort in the night hours when there is no shoulder to cry on. Lord, You are here with the revelation that You are keeping track of all that is going on. Somehow, somewhere, all is known and recorded. In the abyss of emptiness and loneliness, it feels as if a safety rope has been thrown down to me.

========================

From the end of the earth I call to You when my heart is faint;
Lead me to the rock that is higher than I.

(Psalm 61:2 NASV)

Lord, during a seizure, to see Johan shake like a rag doll overwhelms me. It feels like standing on a sandy beach when a wave comes in. The undercurrent washes away the sand from between your toes and disappears from under your feet. I know that I need to get to higher ground. Jesus, You are my rock.

===========================

My soul, wait in silence for God only,
For my hope is from Him.
He only is my rock and my salvation,
My stronghold; I shall not be shaken.
On God my salvation and my glory rest;
The rock of my strength, my refuge is in God.
Trust in Him at all times, O people;
Pour out your heart before Him;
God is a refuge for us.

(Psalm 62:5–8 NASV)

Thank You, Father, that I can pour out my heart before You. You have become my partner. You do not despise my doubts, my fears and my inadequacies. As I pour out my heart, You show me how I can trust in You. You put a firm foundation under my feet again. You know, Lord, how shaken I am. If I look to my own resources, and myself, I know that I cannot survive a day. However, Your Word says that I can trust in You. You are my salvation, my rock, my strength and my refuge. I can trust in You and not be afraid of what tomorrow will bring.

===========================

Blessed be the Lord, who daily bears our burden,
The God who is our salvation.

(Psalm 68:19 NASV)

Thank You, Jesus, that I do not have to carry this alone. I can give You my burdens, not only that of how to help Johan regain his sanity, but also the burden of how to coach the children. My precious little children who are crushed by their father's indescribable presence. They want to talk to him, but he just does not comprehend their world. That gift of being able to step into someone else's experience has disappeared. This weighs heavily on me. I want the children to love and respect their father. This is hard when he cannot remember at the end of the sentence what the beginning was.

=========================

How blessed is the man whose strength is in You;
In whose heart are the highways to Zion!
Passing through the valley of Baca [weeping], they make it a
   spring;
The early rain also pcovers it with blessings.
They go from strength to strength,
Every one of them appears before God in Zion.

(Psalm 84:5–7 NASV)

I feel stuck in the 'valley of weeping'. I need to speak to my heart not to despair, but I grieve over not being known by my husband. It is not a malicious or violent choice. There is no one to blame, but he is gone. The one who captured my heart and made me hope in a life together is gone. I do not have the power to call him back into existence and for this, my heart grieves.

I sometimes wonder if I am to blame for him having to suffer like this. Maybe I should have allowed our pastor to pray that he would pass away during his time in the Intensive Care Unit?

At that time, the promises of hope were still so vibrant in colour, the prayer shield very protective against the insidious arrows of the enemy. Nevertheless, as the days have crept into weeks, into months, I feel that I have maybe chosen the wrong side. It seems too horrible a thought even to admit to myself, let alone speak out to someone else.

Even though Johan's physical shell is being restored, the spark which made him the one for whom my heart longed is gone. How I yearn for a spontaneous hand on my shoulder or a comforting word assuring me that there is light at the end of the tunnel. The 'valley of weeping' seems too wide to cross even in my lifetime.

But there is a promise. A promise that even in the valley, new springs can be dug. Springs of blessing, not only for myself but also enough to give to others.

*You did not choose me, but I chose you
and appointed you to go and bear fruit – fruit that
will last.
Then the Father will give you whatever you ask in
my name.*

(John 15:16)

10

Give What You Have

Nearly a year and a half after the operation, we went back to visit the Youth With A Mission base in Amsterdam, where Johan had taken his Bible school students in earlier days. Floyd McClung, the base director, was one of the spiritual leaders who had come to the hospital to pray with Johan the evening before his operation. Now we sat again with this apostle to urban missions.

Despite Johan's memory limitations and approximately 100-word vocabulary, God gave Floyd eyes of faith to see Johan as someone to whom God had given life back for a purpose. God still had a plan.

Can you imagine how wonderful it was to hear such words of hope? Furthermore, God had already been speaking, and Floyd's comments underlined His message to us. We had just read in the children's Bible a very simple account of the five loaves and two fish. This story had inspired us not to be passive and sit around waiting for life to change. There was something that we needed to do ourselves.

The loaves and fish have been fuel for many sermons.

What spoke to us was the little boy's willingness to give all that he had. Instead of looking at the masses and thinking that his part was too insignificant, he looked to Jesus and believed that He could make something out of nothing.

Dare we be like that little boy and ask God to use us? What did we really have to give Him, anyway? Our lives looked more like crumbs when compared with the past.

But we still loved the Lord.	*'Enough'*
We had hearts filled with compassion.	*'Enough'*
We could extend hands of mercy.	*'Enough'*
We could receive others and bless them with hospitality.	*'Enough'*
We could wash people's feet.	*'Enough'*
We could care for and comfort those with a broken heart.	*'Enough'*

We wanted to make a difference, even if it was a small difference. We did not want to stay in the prison of self-pity, even though it was the most logical place to dwell at that moment. The temptation was to want to wait until everything was restored to how we thought it should be, before stepping out into the unknown. We could only accept this new challenge if we were sure that it was the Lord who was inviting us to come. We asked the Lord in prayer for His guidance.

When we accepted Floyd's invitation to Johan to do a Discipleship Training School by himself in Amsterdam, it was the first of many baby steps forward in faith. A future was being worked on.

Instead of apparent stagnation in our lives, it was as if the water was flowing again. A new perspective had been given. In place of seeing only the past, mourning over all the achievement and accomplishments which seemed gone for ever, there was a tomorrow opening ahead, waiting for us to enter.

Before Johan moved to Amsterdam to do the school, I was overjoyed to discover that I was pregnant.

There had been a promise: I was carrying the promise of so long ago. Although it seemed a human impossibility, this seed of promise stirred Johan's memory of long-forgotten events. From a far-away region, his sense of parental identity with the other three children began to resurface. Slowly, oh so slowly, the moments you share only as parents at the birth of each child carved a way back into his consciousness.

Life was sparking life. Hope was sparking hope. Courage to go on was just a little bit easier to find. Surely there would be a tomorrow. I was carrying that tomorrow.

As with all the children we had received, we wanted to say something about God in the name we chose. Which name would express the journey on which we had been up to this point?

Johan had been reading about the life of Joseph in Genesis. This young man had had dreams, but they too had seemed shattered. His journey took him through enslavement, prison, rejection and then the sudden fulfilment of promises made long ago. It was not coincidental that when Joseph was appointed prime minister over Egypt, he named his second son *Ephraim*. In the midst of Joseph's breakthrough, he acknowledged that 'God had made him fruitful in the land of his affliction'.

Our son was given this name as a prophetic declaration

that fruitfulness would once again characterise our lives. Though, as with most things in life, a timetable was not included. When this would happen was not clear, but that it would happen was sure.

Those who hope in the L<small>ORD</small>
will renew their strength.
They will soar on wings like eagles,
they will run and not grow weary,
they will walk and not be faint.
(Isaiah 40:31)

11

Hope

With each step of the journey, I actually expected a definitive breakthrough to take place. But the reference points of the past were gone. Johan did not just suddenly 'wake up' and recover his leadership gift or speaking abilities or former personality.

My heart ached as I saw how he struggled to find the right words to convey the deep, deep thought on which he had been meditating. The passageway of communication from the heart, via the mind, through the spoken word was clogged. Sometimes we could see on his face that he understood what was going on inside, but he did not understand that we needed more information to know what he was really saying. At other times a cloud would come over his face as he realised that he did not have the vocabulary to paint the picture that was emerging on the screen of his mind.

Yet hope had not faded in my heart that what we had committed to the Lord would take place. He had promised to give us a future and a destiny. I knew that the day Johan died he would be completely healed. Even now, I knew that his spirit had not been touched, in spite of the fact that his mind and body had received considerable damage. The question was, how much could I hope for on this side of eternity?

During the Discipleship Training School (DTS), Johan began to improve. The three-month lecture phase spent under the teaching of the Word of God brought considerable restoration. His vocabulary grew from approximately 100 words to 300 words. The neurologist was impressed that he had made such strides.

Each Friday evening, I would drive to Amsterdam to pick Johan up and take him home to Soest for the weekend. On Sundays, we would join the YWAM community for their afternoon worship service. The children enjoyed being part of an international community.

Due to those first telling signs of restoration, we were encouraged to do the DTS the next year, this time as a family. There were no bridges back to the past. New bricks had to be laid in order to create a new bridge to the future. New training was providing those new bricks.

Financially we were challenged. Through all that had happened up to this point and my own inability to understand all the right Dutch forms to fill out, our income had been reduced to the bare minimum. Taking steps of faith to get some training was imperative, but where was the finance going to come from? The choice had to be made: either look at the visible world with its limitations, or once again ask the Lord for His perspective and strategy.

I started writing to our family and friends and explained the journey that we were on. Slowly, finances began to come in for us to go to Amsterdam and do a school together as a family. In taking this step, Johan had to relinquish his government disability compensation and health coverage and we had to find a private insurance company who would be willing to take us on, given Johan's recent medical history.

How were we able to trust God for these tremendously complicated decisions? How did we know that He would not abandon or desert us? How could we dare take our children on such an adventure?

The basis for this decision went back to the prayer that had been prayed repeatedly.

'Lord, we do not have a plan B. If You do not come through, we will not make it. We have asked for Your guidance and we desire to follow Your leading. Your Word promises that You will never put to shame those who put their trust in You. Jesus, You are our inheritance. Our lives are Yours; show us the way so that we will not be stuck in doubt or uncertainty. We are walking on a road on which we have never been before. We have never heard of others taking these kinds of steps under these circumstances. We choose to put our trust in You. We agree with Psalm 56 where it says, "When I am afraid, I will put my trust in You."

'We acknowledge that it is a rather scary road onto which we are stepping, but we choose to put our trust in You. Your Word says that You are reliable and that You care. You are teaching us to cast our burdens and inadequacies on You. You are teaching us to believe that You are not only the Creator, but You can recreate what has been damaged and destroyed.

'As we take these steps of faith, we ask for divine protection on our children. We love these brave little warriors who have been so loving under such duress. Bless them abundantly and open their eyes to be able to see Your glory. You have an inheritance for them.

Through all of their tears, You want to show them Your comfort and care.

'Give us the courage not to give up. Give us the perseverance to push through to yet one more day.'

Through prayer, the reading of His Word and wise counsel from friends, the Lord began to speak to us during the school about Him wanting us to live permanently in Amsterdam as a family.

It was one thing to do some training in that city, but to move away from the beautiful town of Soest was something I was not convinced was a good idea. Had we not been through enough challenges already? How could our kids grow up to be healthy people living between bricks and concrete? Did they not need grassy fields and trees to give them balanced personalities? Isn't the city, with its spiritual darkness and endless temptations, a place to be avoided at all costs? I remembered that my parents had taken me to post-war Japan when I was a baby. In my mind, that seemed an easier move than contemplating relocation to Amsterdam. Didn't this city of all cities represent everything from which you wanted to shield your children?

I wrote a short article about that time of decision-making, which I would like to share with you. It echoes the struggle I felt about taking the step of moving to the city with a family.

The inner city of Amsterdam forms a hub of intrigue and delight. Tourists, refugees, and pilgrims of every description make their way to this 'Venice of the North'. Its ethnic mixture contains more than 170 major nationalities and countless sub-groupings. This city of refuge has, for centuries, been the destination for those seeking a place where social and religious tolerance would triumph.

Amsterdam was once a haven of refuge, founded on Christian principles. Now it is filled with prostitution, drug trafficking, and addiction; child pornography has found an ample breeding ground along these picturesque canals.

Before joining YWAM, our family asked the Lord where we should live. We felt He said, 'The heart of Amsterdam'. With four young children, my heart's cry was, 'Lord, how can our children grow up to be normal people in the centre of such degradation?'

As I expressed my fear and apprehension to the Lord, the Holy Spirit brought peace and understanding. Only in the centre of God's will is there true safety. With a deep assurance, we knew God was with us. He would be our source of wisdom in raising our children. He is concerned about their well-being.

My fears of raising children here are valid, but the Lord is asking me to look to Him. He gives wisdom to nurture our children to be God-fearing, God-loving people.

In the physical realm, there are many stumbling blocks in a city like Amsterdam. However, the Lord encouraged me to look with a different pair of eyes at the place to which He was calling us.

'Carolyn, you asked Me to lead and guide you. You asked for My perspective and I want to show you how I see the city. I love Amsterdam. I see it as a place of great potential. It is a city of refuge for so many downtrodden and displaced people. They come seeking fulfilment and satisfaction, but look for that in all the wrong places and for all the wrong reasons. Will you be willing to go and share My heart with those who are lost and dying? Will you be My hands and feet to share My love with those whom you meet? It is no wonder, if all My followers abandon the city, that it is so dark. I want to send you there to be My light. My hand will be on your

children, for they too will have an inheritance in what you will be doing.'

Could this really be true?

'But Lord, we are so weak; Johan still does not consistently remember our names and continues to have heavy epileptic seizures. What do we have to offer? We are not powerful or financially on top of things. These are the things that count in the city. How will we make it as a family in such a setting?'

The answer that came was incredible.

'When people look at you and know the journey on which you have been, then they will know that it was I who helped you. Are you willing to allow Me to work through your weakness, insignificance and inabilities in this way? I want to reveal My glory and show My power through you. Are you willing?'

With an invitation like this, the only thing left was to take a step in the direction of our future. The little spark of faith ignited trust to go into the unknown. One of the advantages when acknowledging weakness and limitation is knowing that you can appeal to One who is greater and stronger.

Though the fig-tree does not bud
and there are no grapes on the vines,
though the olive crop fails
and the fields produce no food,
though there are no sheep in the pen
and no cattle in the stalls,
yet I will rejoice in the Lord,
I will be joyful in God my Saviour.

> *(Habakkuk 3:17–18)*

12

Facing Disappointment

When we knew that we were going to be moving to Amsterdam, we asked the Lord for a strategy. In the Bible, there are many examples of God giving clear instructions to those who needed a divine blueprint. Joshua received an unlikely plan as to how to capture Jericho. Who would have guessed that seven days of marching and a thunderous shout would bring down such impregnable walls? Gideon was a self-confessed coward and yet the Lord saw the valiant warrior spirit in him and the heart of obedience to follow His instruction when told to reduce the army before the battle. Imagine a small band of 300 with torches and clay pots as weapons!

As we waited on the Lord in prayer, the plan became clear that we were to join and help in mercy ministries. The YWAM leadership was extraordinary. They received us as a little family, not as a liability. They actually saw potential in us.

Johan's vocabulary, though improved, was still about 300 words at this point. He continued to have frequent seizures as the medication was not helping. Each time he met people, they had to reintroduce themselves to him.

Despite these challenges, there was a depth of communion with Jesus that he had which went beyond words. Johan radiated deep inner peace which can only come when you know that you have significance and worth. Johan knew that Jesus loved and cared for him. And it showed.

A decision was made that Johan would help out with the team that was working with street people. The amazing thing was that this was a perfect fit. Johan did have the ability to listen. Even though his answers were not always fluid in expression or rich in vocabulary, there was a connection born out of brokenness that enabled him to communicate something more of eternity into the here-and-now. In the years following, he led many to the heart of the Father in this way.

Taking these steps to reinvest what he had brought him to the edge of his endurance. He was courageous in daring to step out, not knowing when a seizure would hit. However, once he put himself in a position to give out of what he had, the Lord started to replenish his supply. Not only in the area of communication, but also relationally, Johan was learning once again to build bridges.

During our second year in Amsterdam, Johan started to 'awaken'.

I have had to think deeply about what this really means. Up to this point, Johan's world orientation had been what I had taught and shared with him. In some ways you could say that he was repeating what I had said. With this 'awakening', he began to remember, by himself, who he had been. The reality of his situation began to penetrate his consciousness, and the process left him feeling like a bird with clipped wings. This brought frustration beyond words as a faint memory began to emerge of what it had been like to soar like an eagle.

He remembered his experience of being in the presence of the Lord. Up until this point we had not actually *known* that he had been to meet with Jesus, as he had not been clinically dead. Our friend had had a picture that Johan had gone into the presence of the Lord, but now he began to share this out-of-body experience. His memory of this event was very vivid, but it was hard for him to pin-point when it had occurred. It must have taken place while Johan was in a coma in the ICU, most likely around the time his first seizures started and the anaesthesia was induced. He had no recollection of the actual surroundings of the ICU.

He said that there was a perfect peace and awe in being in the presence of the Lord. There was a knowing that silenced any question or need to ask or to speak. He was prostrate, on his face in worship to the Lord and yet he could see Him. Jesus shone in radiance, but it was not a blinding type of light. His face was not visible. There was an over-whelming lightness and joy in Johan's spirit. This was a place where he wanted to stay. There was a complete sense of fulfilment, of finally coming 'home'. The Lord, however, had other plans. Johan remembers being sent back to his body to fulfil the calling that God still had for him.

Awakening to the reality of the brokenness of his life, remembering how he used to function, and also recalling the utter satisfaction he had felt in the Lord's presence, filled Johan with anger and depression. He felt he could not go on in the bitter disappointment of what his life now was. It seemed that all dignity had been stripped from him.

Instead of a pruning process, it was as if the mighty oak had been axed at its roots.

Epileptic attacks continued to cripple him. He became aware that people knew who he was, while for him, each new encounter with a friend or acquaintance was like meeting with a stranger. He had no recourse but to have basic introductions given time and time again. As a trained commando, someone who could tackle any impossibility and still come out on top, seeing himself in his present state was nearly an impossible burden to bear.

Up until this point, he had not intuitively remembered who he had been. This had made the first four years somewhat 'easier' for him. Now, questions and doubts tormented his spirit. Why did the Lord allow him to continue to live in such a broken state? What honour could this possibly bring to him or God?

Over time he turned to God's Word for consolation for his questions. As he read about Nebuchadnezzar in the book of Daniel, he saw how this king had been humbled and had come to his senses after asking forgiveness from God for demanding an answer to his suffering. Johan recognised in himself that he too was demanding that God give an account of Himself.

It was a profound point of relinquishment when Johan asked the Lord to forgive him for his anger – anger which was based on that deep disappointment with God for allowing him to go on living with so many handicaps. He asked the Lord for grace to live with dignity despite his limitations. He confessed that he did not want to hide behind the problems, but that he wanted God to use what was left of his life for His honour.

Coming to this point of breakthrough in his spirit did not change the circumstances overnight, but what it did do was re-establish faith and hope in his life that the Lord still had a plan. Instead of letting the circumstances dictate his response, Johan embraced the invitation to acknowledge God's goodness and care in the midst of all that was going on.

Several years down the road, the medication that Johan needed for the seizures destroyed his gall bladder. Two operations followed, as the incision was ripped open twice during subsequent seizures. The challenge not to give up, but to press on, was under severe pressure and so became a daily choice. The promise in God's Word remained that there was a future and a hope. Could it possibly be true that the Lord could receive the honour by our persevering, one day at a time?

It was not by their sword that they won the land,
nor did their arm bring them victory;
it was your right hand, your arm,
and the light of your face, for you loved them.
                    (Psalm 44:3)

13

Perseverance

The second part of God's strategy for us as a family in moving to the city was to set up a non-profit foundation and buy a house as a place to offer hospitality to people who were passing through. Given our recent background, this seemed an impossibility.

We had experienced the truth of John 10, that we could hear the voice of the Lord and that He really could speak to us. As we were waiting in prayer, the names of four people we knew came to mind. We wrote them down and then called those people. We presented the plan to have a house of hospitality, a place of refuge in this great city of refuge. It was to be a home where others would feel welcome and receive a little more of God's love.

The first three people we called were very encouraging and challenged us to pursue the idea further. When we called the fourth person, we were overwhelmed by the response. After we had presented the project, this woman shared that the Lord had just been speaking to her about giving a substantial amount of money, although she did not know to whom it was to be given. On hearing from us, she felt that she was to give us this sum of money. The amount would not buy a house, but what it did do was release faith that the Lord was up to something.

As a step of faith, our son Judah, then six years old, came to us with five Dutch guilders in his hand. He said that he knew God was going to give us a house and he wanted to be a part of buying it. Oh, to have the faith of a child!

We presented our plan to the leadership of our church and YWAM. Both groups encouraged us to pursue the project.

The first house that we looked at was beautifully renovated, but the bank was not interested in giving us a mortgage. We had already given notice in Soest and would have to vacate our home within two months. We were convinced that something would happen, as money was now coming in on a regular basis for the proposed house in Amsterdam. We had already set up a non-profit foundation for its acquisition, providing others to hold us accountable in what we were doing. We also needed legal and financial expertise, which we did not have ourselves. A group of amazing friends were willing to back us up and formed a board for us. What is written in Proverbs is true: there is safety in the multitude of counsellors.

The day came when we needed to move from Soest, but we still did not have a place in Amsterdam. All our possessions were stored in a large cargo container and this was parked on the grounds of our home church. The day of the move, it was raining heavily.

Several weeks later, I woke up one morning with a horrible realisation that all our possessions would be covered with mildew because of the rain. We could not unpack everything to air the container, but what we could do was go and walk around the container and ask the Lord to stop the formation of the mildew. This we did and months later, when we finally had a home and unpacked our belongings, on every mattress there was a slight discolouring. It was evident that mildew had begun to grow, but it had stopped! There was not even the faintest musty odour. Everything smelled as fresh as spring.

As city nomads we moved into a couple of rooms in one of the mission buildings. It seemed so incongruous; we knew that something was about to happen, but we did not know when it would take place. After a week, our little tribe had to move down the hall to a couple of other rooms. This move was maybe the most difficult of my life. The resilience in all of us was nearly gone. Although the move could hardly have been over a shorter distance, it felt as if we were displaced refugees.

The question arose: 'Do we have the timing right on this one?' We were attempting something against all odds.

A missionary couple had left for furlough, so we were able to stay in their flat for three months. Because we believed that we were going to be moving to the inner city, we put the children in a school in the heart of the city. This meant commuting daily on the subway.

In the middle of this time of transition, Johan suffered a medication poisoning. One night, during a severe seizure, his brain did not send the signal to his lungs to continue breathing. He started to turn deep purple due to the lack of oxygen. I did not know how to resuscitate him, as his jaw was clamped shut.

I literally screamed out to the Lord for help. The panic of

not knowing what to do to keep my husband alive was all around. Then I suddenly sensed that the Holy Spirit was telling me to resuscitate him through his nose. I did and he started breathing again. Later I learned that this is the official way to give CPR to someone in this condition, but I had not had any former training about it.

As if this were not enough, the mail arriving not too many weeks later included a report that all our post bank cheques had been cashed. We were in the red by many thousands of guilders. Initially I was in such denial that I wanted to call the bank and tell them that they had sent us the wrong statement. The problem, however, was that it was our account. The money for the house was in a special account and was not affected by this, but the implications for us as a family were that we had nothing to live on and the account was blocked until the problem was dealt with. An investigation followed. After three months, it became clear that a bank employee had stolen our cheques and had used all of them. The bank reimbursed us for the debt and the enormous interest that was incurred during the whole process.

Despite all these added traumas, the only word from the Lord was, '*Persevere.*'

One morning in November, we were having a time of prayer. We were facing yet another move, which meant that in one year we had each had eight different beds to sleep in. For all of us, our endurance was wearing thin. We still believed that God was up to something, but we did not have the timetable for when it would happen. For our children's sake, we needed some form of stability. Maybe we should just rent an apartment. Maybe this was not the right time after all.

That morning, however, on 11 November, the Lord spoke to us from Psalm 44:3.

> It was not by their sword that they won the land,
> nor did their arm bring them victory;
> it was your right hand, your arm,
> and the light of your face, for you loved them.

That evening someone called to give us 100,000 Dutch guilders (US $50,000).

The next day, the estate agent informed us that a house had just been placed on the market and that we were the first people to be allowed to visit and look around it.

Together we went to see the house on the Romeinsarm-steeg, a narrow connecting street between two canals, right behind the palace in the inner city of Amsterdam. The ground-floor level was a large garage. There were three floors above it. The house had been built in 1740 and had recently been renovated. It was spacious, with enough rooms for a family of six and the many guests we were anticipating. When we walked up the long flight of stairs from the street to the first floor, we sensed the Lord say that He had been saving this place for us.

Johan went to the bank with his limited vocabulary and explained that we were missionaries and did not have a set salary (only gifts from family, friends and churches), and he asked to apply for a mortgage. What Johan did not know at that moment was that the young man at the counter knew him. He happened to be the boyfriend of one of the young women who used to be in our youth group. He knew of Johan's journey of faith and perseverance. He was able to secure us a mortgage.

On 24 December 1987, we moved into this house of promise. The first thing we did was to walk over the ground floor and dedicate this house to the Lord and to His purposes. We asked that this home would be a place of great blessing to many people. God's timing was perfect, His ways unfathomable.

A generous man will prosper;
he who refreshes others will himself be refreshed.
                                        (Proverbs 11:25)

14

Hospitality

We finally had a home in the inner city. As a family, we were to bless, show mercy and do acts of kindness. Our home was named *De Loofhut*, which is the Dutch name for the Feast of Tabernacles. During this Jewish feast, the people were to remember that they were pilgrims on earth. Our desire was to offer accommodation to other pilgrims who would come our way. The word *loofhut* can also be translated as 'a place of praise'. Our desire was that our home would be a place of joy and praise to God.

Who would these people be to whom we were to minister? We knew that we were not to become a crisis centre for homeless drug addicts, in spite of our earlier work with such people, but as yet it was not clear whom we were to receive into our family.

Yes, this was a family endeavour. All the children had a very significant role to play. In the New Testament, hospitality is included in every list regarding the prerequisites of leadership. Through their involvement in this service, the children would learn some leadership qualities first hand. It would enable them to learn how to share their lives with others.

We were not to entertain people, but we were to welcome them into our lives. Hospitality begins in the heart. It is based on the understanding that the Lord is the Source from which we can give. There was room at the table, in our home, but most significantly in our hearts.

Even though we did not fully understand it in the beginning, generosity would be a major key enabling us to move further on in this life to which God had called us. As generously as we had received, the Lord challenged us to give to others. There were times when I knew that the food I had was not sufficient to feed everyone at the table. I had no extra money to get more provisions and yet everyone who was eating with us got their fill. We would even have leftover food. Sometimes the kids would jokingly ask me not to pray so hard, because they were not particularly fond of leftovers!

Travellers, missionaries, pastors, neighbouring kids, students, unknown friends, stranded tourists – hundreds of people began to come our way. It was not always easy to accommodate so many people on a small budget, but the key was the following prayer: 'Lord, in ministering to the people You bring our way, we do this as an act of worship to You. Your Word says to "offer hospitality to one another without grumbling. Each one should use whatever gift he has received to serve others" (1 Peter 4:9–10). Lord, please provide all that is needed to minister Your love to the people who come through our front door.' With each request we received, we asked the Lord if we were to be part of the solution. Often the answer was yes, although there were times when we had to turn people down.

As we gave out, we were blessed in return. The children were a delight. They had purposed in their hearts not to put on 'company behaviour'. This may have started as a precocious whim, but it turned out to be a blessing. They simply included everyone in their hearts and in the dinner-table conversation. When a group of Romanian pastors, who were staying with us, reached across the table for an item, the kids followed their actions, wanting to save the guests from feeling they had done something impolite.

From the Albanian Minister of Finance to travelling Brazilian students, all were welcome. Each brought their stories with them. It provided a rich storehouse of life experiences in which we were blessed to share.

One day, I received a call from the office saying that a couple were stranded in the city due to a mix-up with their flight and they needed accommodation. Could I help? We already had two guests staying with us, my washing machine was broken, and Johan had gone on a trip, so I felt well within my rights to turn them down. There was a little inner voice, however, which said that I should give this couple our bedroom and I could sleep on a mattress in one of the kids' rooms. I was on the verge of feeling sorry for myself when I realised that this suggestion was a realistic option. Feeling quite sacrificial all the same, I got the room ready.

When the guests arrived, the delightful couple immediately fitted in. Then, to my surprise, the blessing that the Lord did not want me to miss was revealed. Our eldest son had been struggling with dyslexia. The wife of this couple specialised in tutoring dyslexic children. She dedicated her one week in Amsterdam to helping Jozua. What she taught him helped form the breakthrough which later enabled him to go on and finish Dutch university.

I could so easily have missed that blessing. I really did have some valid arguments as to why it would have been too much to take these guests. Through this experience the Lord taught me anew how important it is to ask Him for wisdom and discernment. There is a strong encouragement in Hebrews 13:2: 'Do not forget to entertain strangers, for by so doing some people have entertained angels without knowing it.'

As the years have gone by, we have had the privilege of extending hospitality to literally thousands of people. Sometimes it has meant offering a clean bed and a hot meal; at other times it has meant serving a cup of coffee and having a heart-to-heart chat. Groups have needed a place to get together, prayer meetings have been held, children have come by to play with the Lego and Sam the dog. While drinking afternoon tea together, others have heard and received the love of the Father for themselves.

The Lord showed us what our little loaves and fish looked like. He had taken the crumbs that we had put into His hands and He had multiplied them. He had been looking to see if we were available. He had been looking to see if we would choose Him above our pain and sorrow.

Would we allow His resurrection power to flow through us, thus releasing us from bitterness, despair and self-pity? He showed us that ministering to others was an act of worship to Him. In fact, this was the highest calling that He had placed upon our lives. He wanted to teach us that all we do in word and deed must be done to His honour and glory through the strength that He provides.

I often asked the Lord what difference it made for us to

be here in the inner city of Amsterdam, doing what we were doing. His answer was definitely from a different perspective than my own: *'Choosing to worship Me in the midst of the life you lead brings Me much joy. Having your home as a place where I am honoured and called upon brings Me great delight.'* Seen from His perspective, life's common, everyday experiences were transformed into a sanctuary of fellowship with the Most High God. Our home would become a place where we communed with angels, where supernatural provision had to take place or we would not make it.

As the months melted into years, the biggest miracle was that we had been sustained, cared for and loved. We were so unbelievably rich. Not rich in the sense that the world sees, but rich in the sense that we had been allowed to see the fingerprints of God all over our lives. We had been empowered not to be stuck in the 'valley of weeping'. It had actually turned into a place of springs. Jesus is the Source. His spring never runs dry.

> Blessed is the man who trusts in the LORD,
> whose confidence is in him.
> He will be like a tree planted by the water
> that sends out its roots by the stream.
> It does not fear when heat comes;
> its leaves are always green.
> It has no worries in a year of drought
> and never fails to bear fruit.
>
> (Jeremiah 17:7–8)

It is from this wellspring that we have been able to give. The process of giving has released the provision and, as a side note, has kept our hearts free from the prison of self-pity.

One of the most powerful lessons in the area of hospitality that I have learned was taught me during an outreach that we led to Albania.

Several years ago, we took a missions team to Albania to help with the renovation of a school in a small mountain village. The mayor of this village had received a Bible. He had read it and believed the message that is in it. He asked the missionary who had helped him to understand the Bible if there was a group who could come to get the local school fixed up so that classes could be resumed. We were asked to help facilitate this process. With a group of 35 Dutch young people, we made the long bus and boat trip down to Albania. We had a truck full of practical things like blankets, clothes and shoes to give out to these extremely poor mountain villagers. We also had with us the paint and all necessary items to refurbish the school.

Upon arrival, we were billeted in the local homes. This meant sleeping with ten others in one room, under unique circumstances. Our washing facility was the local creek. All of us were rather stretched solving how to go about our daily business with so little privacy. What overwhelmed all of us, however, was the gracious hospitality extended to us. Often when we think of offering hospitality, it is from a place of abundance. Here we were confronted with extreme poverty but exceptional willingness in the local people to share with us what they had.

One afternoon, the mayor took me to visit the poorest of the poor in the region. We had blankets and other household items to give to whoever needed them, but he wanted me to see first hand how people actually lived. As we made our way over small mountain trails to the little isolated huts, I was at a loss to know how to respond. At every home, I was given the sour milk beverage which is saved for special occasions. The struggle in my heart came from knowing the villagers were giving me their best. I knew that this was something I could not turn down. I felt humbled by their outpouring of hospitality.

After we had visited four or five homes, the mayor told me in advance that we would be visiting the poorest widow as our last stop. I was not prepared for what I encountered. This woman and her four children lived in one very small room with a dirt floor. The cupboards were bare. The children ran around without any shoes, as their mother was unable to afford them. I was offered the only seat, which was a small cot where they slept at night. There was some hustle and bustle as the mother sent the children off with instructions. I realised that they wanted to offer me something to eat or drink, but there was absolutely nothing in the house. Within 15 minutes, the children returned with little ears of roasted corn. I began to protest to the mayor that I really had no need to eat and, moreover, I could not take any of their food as I saw they had none for themselves.

The mayor turned to me and said, 'Carolyn, do not withhold the blessing from them. Don't you remember what the Bible says? "It is more blessed to give than to receive." No one is so poor that he cannot give.'

Completely humbled, I received the small ears of roasted corn as if they were gold. Tears were streaming down my cheeks as I ate. Here, in the most impoverished circumstances, I realised that this widow and her children had grasped an essential lesson. They did not allow their poverty to imprison them. The solution was to pick a few ears of corn, though they had not yet ripened fully, that they might bless. In giving, they were being blessed.

This experience has radically changed how I do things. Whatever I have done in the area of hospitality, I have asked the Lord to help me do it from my heart. My prayer has become, *'Lord, help me not to get hung up on all the outward appearance of things. Let me have the same heart as the Albanian widow who so desired to bless that she gave her all.'*

Those who sow in tears
will reap with songs of joy.
He who goes out weeping,
carrying seed to sow,
will return with songs of joy,
carrying sheaves with him.
          (Psalm 126:5–6)

15

Honouring

After Johan's operation, there were several fundamental choices that I had had to make. I had
realised that one of the keys to our survival as a
family was that we had to do it together. Somehow, some
way, the grief must not consume us. Proverbs 14:1 encouraged me: 'The wise woman builds her house, but with her
own hands the foolish one tears hers down.'

This was not the time to give up or to feel sorry for
myself. There still had to be picnics, bike rides, walks in the
forest and tea parties; cookies (yes, mountains of cookies)
needed to be baked; the kids' friends needed to be allowed
over to spend the night; sports classes needed to be taken;
music needed to be made.

As I had seen clearly from God's Word, the children
needed to honour their father. Even in the condition that
he was in, and with his inability to verbalise his emotions or
feelings very well, the Bible was clear that a blessing would
be theirs if they honoured him.

It was obvious that the children would get their cue from
me on how to do so. Many of my prayer journals are filled

with the tension that this brought. I was carrying a profound sense of disappointment, and the children mirrored this. I knew that I must not shame Johan (Proverbs 12:4), but it was so hard to be his walking dictionary and encyclopaedia. I desperately needed to learn how to hand over my disappointment, leaving it with the One who understood.

A deep prayer grew in my heart for God's help and intervention. I had already prayed for help to stay faithful to Johan. I added another prayer to that, asking to learn how to honour and respect, and ultimately learn to love, this new man I called my husband.

Very early on in our parenting, when our son Jozua was born, Johan and I had decided on some non-negotiable things to tell our children.

- They are wanted. They are not an accident.
- They cannot earn our love or God's love. They already have it and it is unconditional.
- We are committed to praying for them daily.
- We are committed to being their fan club, to championing their destiny.
- We desire to live from a place of mutual forgiveness.

These were to be the pillars in their upbringing. Now they shone out like lights on the road for me. I knew from the past that these had been Johan's heart's desire for the children, so even without further consultation, I could speak these things over the children on behalf of both of us.

I would not be honest if I did not share that frustration often got the better of me. It is a tough task to try to be two people in one. But I so wanted us to make it. I so wanted us not to give up. It meant that I had to be willing to confront my own insecurities. All the wrong foundations or lies in my heart which influenced my reactions needed to be faced. It was so easy to fall back into those old patterns of feeling abandoned and rejected, feeling overwhelmed, or allowing the whimpering voice of self-pity to torment me. These insecurities were based on doubts of God's provision, love and care. In confronting them, I needed to allow the Holy Spirit to change my heart.

We were attempting something that seemed impossible: to enter a place of ministry while seeing Johan's healing take place progressively. My faith was being stretched even further. Would the Lord really carry us through? Would there be a point when Johan consistently remembered tomorrow what he had done today? Would a time come when I no longer feared that an epileptic attack would cripple him and wipe the memory slate blank once again? Could I relax and believe that the children would not have to find their father in a seizure and need to give him first aid?

God in His mercy met me on this road and brought healing to my heart and mind. He taught me how to trust and how to let go of the patterns that had nearly crippled me along the way. One of the deepest revelations was of God's unconditional love for me. I did not have to perform to get His attention. If His eye was on the sparrow, how much more was His eye on me?

In later years, as the children were processing their own grief and sadness at growing up with a father who did not really know them, I had to share with them the reality of the choices that we had faced. In working through some of the more difficult issues of life, it always feels better, for a while, if we can blame someone else for life's circumstances.

The reality for us was this: Johan could have passed away, or I could have left him, or he could have stayed an invalid looking out of the window – or we took the steps that we did, even though the territory we entered was uncharted and overwhelming at times. We had made progress, but after moving to the city everything did not suddenly change or improve. The children had to come to terms with the fact that they had a father who was different from the fathers other kids had. They had to learn to dig deeper to see the treasure that was before their own eyes.

We did have a strong sense of family and there was a bond of comradeship and fun that still knits us together. We truly enjoy each other's company. In recent years, I have had to ask each child for forgiveness for how, in my good intentions, I was too strict and sometimes out of balance during their formative years. Much has been written about the 'fatherless generation'. It is easy to be caught up in a spiral of self-pity, bemoaning all the lost opportunities. There is a place for grief. Nevertheless, it is also important to make the choice not to remain stuck, camping out in the 'valley of weeping'. The Lord does heal the broken-hearted. His comfort and reconciliation are available. His invitation to come and receive from Him stands.

I am proud of each of our children and how they have made their way through this period. They are all valiant, God-honouring young adults. They have their own stories to tell. Their emotional journeys have not always been easy, but they have not been sideswiped or demolished by self-pity and anger. Both are choices; they do not just happen. The children have learned not to let the weed of bitterness grow in the garden of their lives. I am grateful for this. I have also had to learn how to let go and not justify myself or my responses or reactions, but allow them to live their own journeys.

Maybe the hardest part of this has been for them to come to a place of forgiveness. Johan was not consciously an absentee father; he was not abusive or irresponsible. His absence was in most part due to factors beyond himself. In talking about the past, Johan has said that there are several years of complete blankness as far as his memory is concerned. When he began to awaken, he lacked the vocabulary to communicate what he saw and felt. As time progressed, he told of how hard it was to communicate deeply. If he tried to formulate a complicated thought, it often triggered an epileptic attack. He grieves over the years that seem to have been lost. From the depth of his being, he has prayed that somehow the children would know that he truly loved and cared for them and was always tremendously proud of them.

As Johan has healed and regained much of what was lost, the process of restoration with the children has been profound and deep. There has been a fulfilment of the promise in Malachi 4:6: 'He will restore the hearts of the fathers to the children and the hearts of the children to their fathers.'

Show me your ways, O Lord,
teach me your paths;
guide me in your truth and teach me,
for you are God my Saviour,
and my hope is in you all day long.
       (Psalm 25:4–5)

16

Forgiveness

Living in the city of the grand Dutch master Rembrandt, I have learned much from observing his paintings. His mastery in portraying light is in direct relationship to his use of shadows. The attention of the observer is immediately drawn to the light. In telling our story, I have attempted not to emphasise the darker side of the journey, but only to refer to it so that the attention will go to the light. This is why I would like to share further lessons from the school of forgiveness.

Maybe one of the hardest parts of the journey of life is to learn how to live from a place of forgiveness. Remembering how much I have been forgiven should enable me to be quick to extend forgiveness to others. My pride generally gets in the way, however, and this is why taking offence happens so easily. We had two major opportunities in which we had to learn this life lesson at a deeper level.

The first situation was when our 'home church' split. Several things had happened to cause friction within the leadership team, which eventually led to part of the congregation splitting off and starting a new church. The division had nothing to do with us personally, but personal feelings of taking offence led us to join the group that had split off. During our time at the DTS, however, the Lord brought conviction that reacting out of pain and anger never serves His purposes. He challenged us to humble ourselves and go back to our former home church. We did. What He taught us through this was that we could appeal to Him who is our righteous Judge for help. When we respond in humility, He will bring healing and restoration. Even now, many years later, we still have warm and strong ties to that church.

This lesson of living from a place of forgiveness was magnified many times over several years later, when Johan was asked to step down from his position working with the street people, as he was considered inadequate to continue what he was doing. Johan was devastated. The rejection was overwhelming to him. He was aware of his broken body, yet he tried not to let that limit him. How could other Christians treat him like this when they knew the journey he was on? It seemed incredibly unfair and cruel.

I was desperate. Where was justice and who would plead our case? Who would mediate and why didn't they give us the benefit of the doubt? And yet . . . I so understood. The brokenness of his speech and understanding still called for a lot of patience and grace to be able to decipher what he was saying. It was something the homeless people and junkies he was working with didn't seem to mind too much. Maybe because of his brokenness he was in a way like them, yet there was hope in his spirit that they wanted to hear more about. And they saw it. Why couldn't the others see it? It was a heart-wrenching situation which nearly crushed us. What had started as a journey of hope against hope now seemed to have come to a dead end, with our hope being dashed to pieces.

In the place of agonising prayer, the Lord spoke again through 1 Peter 2:23. We could entrust ourselves 'to him who judges justly'.

Even though for the moment it seemed very unjust, our response would determine our future and that of the children. We knew we had to submit ourselves and also our pain and questions to the One who rules all. Boy, was this hard! We also knew that it was God who ruled our lives and that though His ways are not our ways, His plans are for good. There must be something else in store for us.

From Ephesians 4:1–3 we were encouraged to 'live a life worthy of the calling you have received . . . make every effort to keep the unity of the Spirit through the bond of peace'.

The reality was that not everyone understood the depth of the pilgrimage on which we had been, and there were others who were not interested. The Lord's invitation to us was to give Him this load and allow Him to sort it out.

Was this being too passive? Absolutely not! Time has proven that the Lord's ways always produce life. It is possible to lash out in response and feel vindicated, but it never produces lasting fruit. Relinquishment, that word that goes so deep, that word that we have had to deal with so often on this road – that word represents the difference between life and death. Letting go and letting God. I am not really good at defending myself, but I do have a Friend who is equipped for the job.

He would remind me that in the same way that I forgave others, He would forgive me (Matthew 6:12–14). He

instructed me that if I did not forgive after I have been forgiven so much, I would be imprisoned to those to whom I
did not extend forgiveness. Yes, God is a righteous Judge. I
can appeal to Him to open my prison doors, even though
they may be of my own making, for an unforgiving spirit
will eventually form a prison around my own soul.

Forgiveness is like taking a bath. I must acknowledge the
fact that I am in need of cleansing. I accept responsibility
for my part in making the situation so broken. I also
acknowledge that God's perspective of a situation is very
different from the way I see it. I ask for His mediation.

God is a Redeemer. When Johan chose to forgive and to
serve, God brought him to another level of fruitfulness in
his life. When it became impossible to continue in one area,
another area of ministry opened up. From this point on, his
speaking ability improved in leaps and bounds. As he
waited on the Lord, God showed him how to use his journey of brokenness as a tool of instruction. He started giving
team-building training. After this ordeal, Johan also
improved in regard to the regularity of his epileptic seizures.
They became so infrequent that he got medical approval to
be able to drive a car again.

Over the years, living from the position of forgiveness has
preserved us as a family. It took the pressure off us trying to
act as if we had everything worked out. We could acknowledge our shortcomings and be the recipients of the forgiveness that we desired from others. Releasing forgiveness
enabled us not to be stuck, but to move on in life.

One of the fundamental principles we were learning was
that God will ask us to give an account only of what we ourselves have done with His grace while on earth. For whatever

anyone else does to us, His grace is available. Jesus' words in Revelation 3:11 stood as an encouragement to seek restitution and not be caught in the pettiness of unforgiveness and interpersonal conflicts: 'I am coming soon. Hold on to what you have, so that no one will take your crown.'

We still had a future; God had given a promise. We didn't know how this revival, which God had initially spoken of, was going to pan out, but God says in His Word that though all this may wither and fade, the Word of the Lord will stand firm. We were determined to do all we could to stay true to His calling and were excited about what He would do, in our lifetime or the next.

Trust in the L<small>ORD</small> with all your heart
and lean not on your own understanding;
in all your ways acknowledge him,
and he will make your paths straight.
                              (Proverbs 3:5–6)

17

Trust

I have often been asked what happened to me during this journey. I'd had dreams and promises for my life. What happened to the fragments with which I was left?

The most significant thing that I was learning was to wait on the Lord, trusting Him for the right season of release in my life. All of us battle at one time or another regarding the issue of significance. We want our lives to count for something bigger than ourselves. I'd had to relinquish my dreams of 'ministry' and do what my hand found to do.

I remember about six months after Johan's operation I had cried out to the Lord and told Him that I needed some sort of mental exercise, to save me from slowly suffocating under the impossibility of conversing with Johan. I sensed that the Lord encouraged me to take up something that I had always wanted to do: to study Russian! This may seem quite illogical, but when growing up in Japan I had studied Russian history and literature, and as a 17-year-old I had travelled on part of the Siberian Railway on my roundabout journey to the States to attend university. The classes I consequently attended did not make me an expert in this beautiful language, but they gave me a healthy mental challenge to tackle, and helped me not to be consumed by the tremendous load I was carrying at home.

Later, when we joined YWAM, which is vibrant with opportunities for service, the circumstances of having four small kids and a husband with Johan's recent medical history still did not allow me the luxury of release into my own ministry. I knew that the Lord was sustaining me. He had proved that so often. He had given me strategies on how to survive, but He wanted to take me further than just survival. He wanted to teach me how to live as a precious daughter of the heavenly Father, even if I did not have any other area through which others could see my value.

During our early years in Amsterdam, I still had a toddler and I decided to coordinate a crèche for the small ones. In this way, mums could have a free morning to be involved in other areas. I purposely do not write 'to be involved in ministry', as the Lord clearly showed me that investing in your own or other people's children is a ministry in itself. The repercussions of this involvement can often be seen for years to come. I still have friendships with those who were formerly in the crèche!

When Ephraim started kindergarten, I became a minibus taxi driver. Our family had been given a nine-seater van, which enabled me to drive eight children from the centre of Amsterdam to the south-eastern part of the city where Christians had established an evangelical elementary school. To take the subway every day was too expensive. Also in those days, the subway was still one of the primary areas where hard drugs were used and sold. It was not uncommon to find discarded needles on the station platform.

The six years that I drove – three hours a day, five days a week, and four weeks a month for ten months a year – were an investment. I was aware of the fact that it was a way of blessing the children of the city. In my years of doing this, a total of 30 different children travelled with me.

A small book written by Brother Lawrence called *Practising the Presence of God* encouraged me. This medieval monk learned how to worship while scouring pots and pans at his sink in a monastery. That was his training ground; mine was the rush-hour traffic around a major urban centre. The erratic driving behaviour of my fellow road-users was not helpful for my stress levels. It definitely offered me a spectrum of opportunities to work on my attitude. Believe me, it was not always easy. However, when I saw how the children thrived on this special time together in the car, I knew that it was worth it. I had music tapes of artists that they liked. They would sing along with the music at the tops of their voices. To this day, Michael W. Smith's early songs remind me of the motorway around Amsterdam.

At a given point, I was asked to become a board member of this elementary school. It was a position that I enjoyed and I fulfilled the responsibility for three years. I could see the bigger picture and the need to lay a firm biblical foundation so that the school would grow to become a significant influence in society.

In 1993 I joined the King's Kids year team as a part-time member of staff. King's Kids is a child- and youth-orientated YWAM outreach programme, which uses the performing arts in evangelism. Roechama and Judah were part of the team, I helped behind the scenes, and Ephraim came along too, joining the group when he was old enough. It was a commitment of one complete weekend per month for a year.

I realised this was a key investment, not only for our children, but also for me. Earlier, when Johan became sick, I'd had to lay down for an indefinite season my dreams of working with young people. Now, being a part of the King's Kids team helped resurrect that dream and gave me hope that more opportunities would come my way to mentor, coach and teach again. I was involved in this ministry for six years.

In 1995 I had a very significant dream. When I woke up, I knew that there was something specific I was to do to prepare for a future activity. I asked the Lord for details of what I was to do. His answer was that I should take up training as a translator/interpreter.

I signed up for a three-year programme, which I had to complete in two years. In between my family responsibilities (among other things I was still reading books out loud to Johan and the children, and did so for 15 years!), guests (we continued to have many hundreds pass through our door), driving to school with my little tribe, and YWAM commitments (from 1990 I interpreted regularly in the various training schools), I read dictionaries and studied grammar books. The course I was taking was geared towards European Union level translation. It gave me the tools that I knew I needed for whatever the Lord had said was coming.

One day, in the midst of interpreting at a Christian conference, it suddenly dawned on me that I was doing exactly what I had always wanted to do during my studies at university. I had always aspired to be a UN interpreter. I never achieved that goal, but it struck me now that I was interpreting at an even higher level. I was interpreting for the King of kings. The realisation filled me with joy.

It is amazing how it is possible to be busy with your own thoughts while interpreting someone else's words. What came next to my mind was actually more a question that the Lord posed to me. His words to me were: *'Carolyn, do you know where this gift of interpreting was formed? In the years that you have been teaching Johan how to speak Dutch again, I have used the process to enable you to learn Dutch at a deeper level than most foreigners are required to do. It is My gift to you. It is a pearl of great value, born out of the tears that you have shed in this process.'*

I nearly burst out crying when this revelation hit me. Thankfully, I managed to restrain myself, as it had nothing to do with what the speaker was saying. The Lord was giving me treasures, unspeakable riches. Who could ever imagine that anything redemptive could have come from the frustration of teaching Johan how to speak again? My heart bubbled over with gratitude.

Since then, interpreting has become an experience of 'dancing with words'. I love the process because I have been able to glimpse what was needed to form this treasure in me.

It is also a way of serving others. We all have a heart language. We can intellectually understand words or concepts in many languages, but it does not always affect the heart. Being an interpreter enables me to facilitate someone in hearing the words at this heart level.

For example, I was recently interpreting at a conference. It is not always appropriate to translate a prayer the speaker may pray out over someone. On this occasion, however, I sensed the nudge of the Holy Spirit to interpret the prayer. I knew that the person who was being prayed for understood

English perfectly well, so it was not an issue of the intellect. The moment I started to interpret into Dutch, the man burst out crying and the healing took place. The prayer reached his heart.

In 1998 the director of YWAM Amsterdam invited me to join his leadership team. When I took up the responsibilities it required, I knew that it was to be a four-year commitment, as this time the Lord had given me an exact timetable. Did I feel adequate for the challenge? Hardly! However, the Lord saw my heart. He knew that I was willing to learn and that I wanted to serve Him in this way. He was inviting me to another level of training. He was showing me how faithful He is to respond to the desires of my heart.

The Lord has taken the little crumbs that I gave Him in trust. As I waited for His timing, the miracle of increase had everything to do with Him. His invitation to me was to trust, to wait, and to position myself in such a way that the multiplication could take place through me. The following verse has been my banner on this journey: 'Let us not become weary in doing good, for at the proper time we will reap a harvest if we do not give up' (Galatians 6:9).

Through the blessing of the upright a city is exalted.
(Proverbs 11:11a)

18

The Faithfulness of God

The path Johan and I are on is not what we would have chosen. Yet as we walk on it, one more step, one more day, we are living proof that God is good and that He will not shame those who put their trust in Him. We have seen the goodness of the Lord in the land of the living. Has it been an easy road? No. Has it been worth it? Yes!

If the Lord could extend His hand of mercy to us, helping us as a family to survive the valley where life's dreams were shattered, and bring us to a place of springs where His promises are being fulfilled, we can be certain that He will have compassion on those in need around us.

I have only mentioned in passing the activities in which we are now involved. Otherwise, our story may seem all about getting back to 'business as usual'. On the contrary, this pilgrimage has been about learning how to draw deeper from the Source. The Source is Jesus. When all else was stripped away, we had to get back to the essentials, the 'one thing needful'. The Source of all essentials, the one solid Rock in the storm, the one hope of life in the valley of the shadow, was always, is always, Jesus. His faithfulness in our lives has built faith in ways we never dreamed.

His faithfulness has given us hope, not only for ourselves and for those around us, but also for the beautiful, prodigal city of Amsterdam. Curiously, the local nickname of the city is an old Jewish word, *Mokum*, meaning 'Source' or 'the Place'. Our prayer is that, because of our own journey in discovering the one true Source, we will be used to help others in this city to find that Source of life also. We pray that when people read about this journey, they will be encouraged that nothing is impossible with God.

Epilogue

The gold frame and the shattered glass were replaced long ago. What had seemed then like an irreparable, irredeemable tragedy has proved to be the makings of an invaluable journey. The process touched each of us deeply. We never got back to what we had been. But it has not been a question of going back; rather, it has been one of transformation and growth, which was preceded by pruning and came without a timetable.

I remember with clarity the first time Johan was once again strong enough to romp around on the floor with the children. They all rolled over their dad like overgrown puppies, happy to measure their strength against the one whose strength they wanted as their plumb line.

Johan has regained his identity, his memory of the past and a large portion of his vocabulary. The wound has healed, but the scar is still visible. Over the years he has seen the brokenness of his body and mind and the effect it has had on his life. He has found ways not merely to cope, but to live. In recent years, however, he has become increasingly aware of the effect all of this has had on the children and on me. This has been a bitter pill to swallow. He loves us so dearly, and to realise that we have been marked by this journey cuts deep. He gladly would have paid the price himself. Embracing this reality is also part of the journey, however, and so rather than grieving the past he turns his energy to show us he cares and joins dreams for the future.

As he has 'awakened', I have been struck by his extraordinary courage to persevere. A man of lesser character would have given up years ago. His humble integrity in wanting to remain faithful to the Lord and his desire to finish what the Lord has for him in life are an inspiration to many.

He has become an avid student not only of the Bible, books and magazines, but has even taken on my quirk of reading dictionaries and idiom books! He always carries a notepad to jot things down as an aide to his memory.

His passion is still to share the gospel with others. This has been the power that has given him a second chance at life. It remains his greatest joy and delight to introduce people to the Father who can heal all of life's deepest wounds. The message that he now gives is much deeper than it was before. He is quick to listen. Often if an answer is not immediate, it means that he is asking advice from the One who really does understand all.

Authentic memories have returned. For example, one morning while eating breakfast, he pulled out one of the spoons from our teaspoon collection. He began to explain that it had been a wedding gift and part of a breakfast set for us as a honeymoon couple. He reminisced about the melt-in-your-mouth scones that I had baked. Believe me when I say there was not a dry eye at the table as Johan carried us back in time to an event long forgotten.

Johan is still gifted with his hands. He uses his engineering abilities as the Technical Director of one of the YWAM facilities. Planning, organising and managing assets are part of his daily responsibilities. Who would ever have thought that this level of restoration was possible?

The children and I feel very secure in Johan's love. Recently he and our boys were at a men's conference. They were all asked to capture what their earthly father was like. They did their best to describe Johan in one profound sentence: 'He is someone who has authority in what he says and does, but with a deep gentleness and meekness which is the complete opposite of weakness.'

One of the elements of life that Johan has been very successful in holding on to is his dignity. He knows that he is loved. He knows that he has intrinsic value, for the One who held him fast so that he would not slip into oblivion is also the One who pronounced over his life, 'You are My workmanship, created in Christ Jesus to do the works that I have ordained for you before the foundation of the world' (see Ephesians 2:10). This has freed Johan from the inner striving which characterises so many men. He has a solid, quiet confidence that 'it is well with his soul'.

It is difficult to capture in words the depth of his character. There are echoes of the past that come back to us, but a new dimension has been added. It has been the result of a deep communion with the Father. When Johan speaks, people listen. His words do not come cheaply, nor are they empty chatter.

All that has been undertaken up until now has been in the realm of the impossible. The only explanation is the intervention of the One who can turn water into wine, calm the stormy tempest and make blind eyes see again.

I have been asked many times, 'What happened with you and Johan. . .?'

Such a miracle took place that a deep, cherishing love was rekindled between us. It did not happen overnight and many choices had to be made in order to re-embrace the person that Johan had become.

He has made a huge effort to get to know me again. He now even remembers the colour of flowers that I love. This may seem insignificant, but to me it means that he has 'come back'. It is strange how important these little signs of acknowledgement are to a person.

I have had to grow up in this process as well. What I mean here is that I have needed to let go of a demanding spirit, of wanting to get back right now all that I had before the operation in fun, love, humour and togetherness. I needed to hold on to the perspective that what was transpiring before my eyes had more to do with eternity than with the here-and-now. As my expectations were re-aligned, they enabled me to grow to appreciate and love the Johan that has returned. He is courageous, noble and valiant, and has persevered against all odds.

* * *

There are several things that have been helpful for us, as we have observed how this city was built. Amsterdam grew up around the swampy mouth of the Amstel River. The foundation of every building was actually on top of long wooden piles, pounded deep into the sand and mud. Today the same method is followed, using strong metal pillars. Without these pillars, a building would simply sink. Like the buildings in this city, we have needed some strong supporting pillars in our lives. In closing, I would like to share these with you. In the midst of the pain and pressure, these pillars have stood firm, upholding us and helping to transform our lives.

Be a worshipper

Nothing can separate us from the love of Christ. Sorrow, grief and disappointment are strong enemies of the soul. They can be destroyed by worshipping the Lord and focusing on the love that He has revealed to us. When we worship we are given the opportunity to practise on earth what we will be doing for eternity.

Be a person of faith

Without faith, it is impossible to please God. The Lord commends and rewards faith. As we see, hear and respond to the truth of His Word, we build and strengthen our faith.

Be grateful

Gratitude shatters the stronghold of discontentment. It enables us to see the flowers growing between the cobblestones of life.

Be holy

Our journey on earth is about the heart and who we will be in eternity. The Lord is first and foremost concerned about our character rather than our actions, as He knows that character affects what we do. He has the power to help us keep our heart clean and pure before Him. 'Blessed are the pure in heart, for they will see God' (Matthew 5:8).

Be a forgiver

Forgiveness is a choice that we can make, in spite of what our emotions are doing. Jesus admonishes us to forgive seventy times seven times. In other words, we are not to keep an account of wrongs that have been inflicted on us, but we are to give them consistently to the One who judges justly.

Be kind

It is the kindness of the Lord that brings us to salvation. We must be watchful as to how we use our mouths. The mouth is a source of either blessings or curses. Ask yourself: What am I saying? Am I agreeing with God with my words, or with the enemy of my soul? Before speaking, remember to think. Ask yourself: Is what I am about to say

> thoughtful?
> helpful?
> inspirational?
> nice?
> kind?

Be hospitable

To be hospitable means to serve. This is a leadership quality. Jesus Himself said that He came to serve and that we are to follow His example.

Be generous

When we know who our Source is and how He loves and cares for us, the natural response will be to give. No one is too poor to be able to give something. All of us have more in our hands than we think. What are your loaves and fish? What are your crumbs?

Be a person of hope

Hope is anchored in who God is and the promises that He has made. When we put our trust in Him, He has promised never to leave us or forsake us. Whatever takes place in our lives, He does have a bigger picture. He desires to show us how it all fits into His eternal design for us. Life is so much more than just the few years that we live here on earth. Live this life in view of eternity.

Be a person of prayer

Commune with the Most High. He longs to have fellowship with you. He desires to reveal His heart, His strategies and His solutions to you. The promise stands true: no one who puts his or her trust in Him will be put to shame.

* * *

These 'pillars' concern lifestyle issues. They have been discovered in the pressure of what we have been through and, as we have held to them, they have helped restore our lives.

They have protected the Source in my heart from being polluted by bitterness, ungratefulness and discontentment. All such qualities deny the truth. I have asked the Lord to help me keep the wrinkles in my face soft as I lean with assurance on the truth that my heavenly Father is good and does all things well.

One point to remember, however: a timetable is not included on the journey.

They overcame him
by the blood of the Lamb
and by the word of their testimony;
they did not love their lives so much
as to shrink from death.

(Revelation 12:11)